SECRETS OF THE NEW CASINO GAMES

**Let it Ride· Caribbean Stud · Pai Gow Poker · War
Spanish 21 · Red Dog · 3 Card Poker · Sic Bo · Pai Gow**

SECRETS OF THE NEW CASINO GAMES

Let it Ride· Caribbean Stud · Pai Gow Poker · War
Spanish 21 · Red Dog · 3 Card Poker · Sic Bo · Pai Gow

Marten Jensen

Cardoza Publishing

ABOUT THE PUBLISHER

Cardoza Publishing is the foremost gaming and gambling publisher in the world with a library of almost 100 up-to-date and easy-to-read books and strategies. These authoritative works are written by the top experts in their fields and with more than five million books in print, represent the best-selling and most popular gaming books anywhere.

*To my dear wife, DeAnna, for her continued support
and for her fine editing skills that helped make this a better book.*

Illustrations by Dylan Bourdages

FIRST EDITION

Library of Congress Catalogue Card No: 00-131795
ISBN: 1-58042-024-9

Write for your free catalogue of gaming and gambling books,
advanced strategies and computer games.

CARDOZA PUBLISHING

P.O. Box 1500, Cooper Station, New York, NY 10276
Phone (718)743-5229 • Fax (718)743-8284
E-mail: cardozapub@aol.com
www.cardozapub.com

TABLE OF CONTENTS

I. INTRODUCTION

This book covers nine of the most popular new casino games: Let It Ride, Caribbean Stud Poker, Three Card Poker, Pai Gow Poker, Spanish 21, Pai Gow, Red Dog, Sic Bo, and War, and not only shows you how to play these games, but also provides you with the best strategies available to beat them!

The first five games – Let It Ride, Caribbean Stud Poker, Three Card Poker, Pai Gow Poker, and Spanish 21 – are described in detail, including the complete rules of play, the best wagers to make, the values of different hands, and the odds of getting pat hands. Numerous charts and tables display information on all the bonus and progressive payouts. The expert strategy advice provided for each game helps players reduce the house edge to a bare minimum. In addition, simplified but effective strategies have been devised for the casual and recreational player.

The latter four new casino games – Pai Gow, Red Dog, Sic Bo, and War – are described in lesser detail mainly because they are either not very popular, are not good games for most people to play, or don't appear to have much long-term staying power. However, we will show the basics of playing and winning at these four games anyway.

In all, you'll learn how to play and win at nine casino games in this book, so let's move on now and see what these new games are all about!

THE HOUSE EDGE

In many cases, the casino's edge is not unreasonable; however, to get the house percentage down as far as it will go requires the use of proper playing strategy.

The following chart will show you how the new games compare to the traditional games:

House Percentage - Casino Games			
GAME	TYPE	CONDITIONS	HOUSE %
Blackjack	traditional	card counting	-0.2 to -1.2
Pai Gow Poker	new	banker (5% rake on winning hands)	-0.2 to -0.4
Blackjack	traditional	basic strategy, single deck	0.1
Blackjack	traditional	basic strategy, 2-6 decks	0.4 to 0.6
Craps	traditional	pass, come, 2X odds	0.6
Spanish 21	new	perfect strategy	0.8
Baccarat	traditional	banker (5% rake on winning hands)	1.2
Baccarat	traditional	player	1.4
Craps	traditional	pass, come, no odds	1.4
War	new	do not play ties	2.9
Three Card Poker	new	pair plus side bet	2.3
Pai Gow Poker	new	player (5% rake on winning hands)	2.5 to 2.8
Roulette	traditional	single-zero wheel	2.6
Three Card Poker	new	perfect strategy	3.4
Let It Ride	new	perfect strategy	3.5
Casino Red Dog	new	perfect strategy	3.5
Roulette	traditional	double-zero wheel	5.3
Caribbean Stud	new	perfect strategy	5.3
Craps	traditional	crapless; pass/come, no odds	5.4
Craps	traditional	field	5.6
Craps	traditional	big 6 or 8	9.1
War	new	play ties	17.0

Negative numbers under HOUSE % indicate the player has the edge!

For those games where players can make strategic choices, the house percentages shown previous are largely based on mathematically-perfect playing strategies. The negative percentages for the first two games listed indicate that they can have a positive expectation of winning for the player.

The house percentage or house edge is the profit the casino makes on the money that a player risks on a game. For instance, if the house edge is 5%, you will lose $5 out of every $100 that you bet. Over the long-term, this is a statistical certainty and the percentages listed above only apply if you play the game using the best strategy. If your playing strategy is poor, the house will get a lot more.

THE NEW CASINO GAMES
Some of the new casino games are actually variations of older games (Pai Gow Poker) while others are creatures of computer technology (Spanish 21). All of these games have been extensively analyzed by their developers to be sure that there is no way to compromise the casino take, either by using a unique playing strategy or by counting cards. They are truly games of the computer age.

TRADITIONAL TABLE GAMES
The traditional table games played in most casinos were invented hundreds of years ago and then evolved over time until they reached their present form. The modern versions of blackjack and craps, where the casino acts as banker, have been around for almost 100 years. While games such as roulette, baccarat, and poker are more than 150 years old.

When these games were originally devised and refined, computers did not exist, so the odds of winning were calculated manually by mathematicians employed by the gaming operators. Much of the playing strategy was developed by intuition and experience. This worked fine for the casinos until almost 40 years ago when some smarties began using computers to develop improved playing strategies.

Gambling hall operators do not like games in which they have a narrow edge. If blackjack were invented today, most casino operators would reject the game as soon as they saw the result of a computer analysis. However, blackjack has become such a universal and ingrained part of the gambling experience that it would be impossible for the casinos to eliminate it. Instead, the casino industry has taken advantage of computer technology to invent a few new table games. With the possible exception of Pai Gow Poker, these new casino games have been thoroughly analyzed by computer before they were introduced on the casino floor to be sure that the casino's profit margin cannot be overcome.

WAGERING ETIQUETTE

Casino table games have unwritten rules of behavior that are followed as a matter of courtesy to the dealer and the other players. These rules are primarily designed to avoid misunderstandings and to keep the game moving smoothly.

When you first plop your behind down at a table, you will need to *buy in*. If you brought chips from another game at that casino, you can play with those; however, you cannot use chips that you brought in from a different casino. In Nevada, real currency can be played at most table games. If you toss a bill on the bet circle, the dealer will call out (for the floor person to hear), "Money plays." If you win your money bet, you will be paid off with casino chips.

To buy in, place your money on the layout; never hand it to the dealer. The dealer will not convert your cash until the current hand is concluded, so don't think she is ignoring you. If you lay out a large bill, it will be entirely converted into chips; the dealer cannot make change. You may, however, ask for specific denominations of chips. When you quit playing and are ready to change your chips back to cash, you have to do that at the cashier's cage.

When approaching a table, check the small plaque that shows the minimum and maximum bets before sitting down—especially if you are playing at $5 or $10 levels. There are many tables with $25 and $100 minimums. Buying in with a 50-dollar bill at a 100-dollar table might be a little embarassing.

No matter which game you are playing, at the start of each hand you must put up one or more bets. If you are slow in doing this, the dealer will gently remind you, but it will also hold up the game. Once the dealer starts distributing the cards, you may not touch your original bet(s). If you do, you will be admonished. This is because one method of cheating is to change the amount of the bet after seeing how good a hand was dealt.

The above rules are general and apply to all table games. Every different type of game also has some unique rules of its own. These additional rules will be covered in the chapters on the specific games.

A FEW WORDS ABOUT STRATEGY

Information on the best playing strategy is provided for each of the games covered in this book. In most cases, both a simplified strategy and a perfect or best strategy are provided. The simplified strategies give results that very closely approximate the perfect strategies and, in any case, are better than using no strategy at all or just playing by intuition.

If you would rather play by intuition, you don't really need this book, but you will need a fat wallet.

The purpose of the strategies is to keep you playing as close to the theoretical minimum house edge as possible. In other words, if the house edge for a particular game is given as 3% and you correctly apply the strategy, you should lose $3 for every $100 that you risk. This is a *long-term average,* and may not apply to short playing sessions. During short playing sessions, the luck of the cards is usually the dominant factor.

If you sit down at a table and start losing hand after hand, you may think, "This strategy is not working for me—I need to do something different." As bad as it looks, however, if you stray from the correct strategy, you will probably be worse off. Actually, you should leave the table. Of course, the reverse could also happen: your first few hands are all winners. This, also, cannot be attributed to the playing strategy, but is the result of normal fluctuations. Regardless of short-term vacillations, in the long run you are always better off when you stick to the statistically-correct strategy.

A NOTE ON PAYOFFS

When a payoff is described as *even money*, that is the same as a payoff of 1 to 1. In other words, if you wager $5 and win, you will be paid an additional $5. In the game of War, for example, when you make a side bet that you and the dealer will tie, the payoff is 10 to 1. If you risk $5 on that wager and win, you get to keep your original bet and will be paid an additional $50.

Occasionally, you may see a payoff stated as 3 *for* 1 instead of 3 *to* 1. On a 3 to 1 payoff, if you wager $5 and win, you will be paid $15 *and* get to keep your original bet. If the payoff is stated as 3 *for* 1, you will also be paid $15, but will lose your original bet. A payoff of 3 for 1 is equivalent to a payoff of 2 to 1. This is a little deception that doesn't fool professionals, but can easily mislead the casual gambler.

A NOTE ON THE GLOSSARY & THE STRATEGY CHARTS

Whenever you come across an unfamiliar term, be sure to look it up in the Glossary at the back of the book. Browsing the Glossary can be enlightening. Some familiar terms may be defined differently than you would have thought.

If you would like to reproduce some of the strategy charts in the book, the Strategy Charts chapter is the place to go. All the simple strategies and most others are replicated here for your convenience in copying. By opening this book flat on a flat-bed copier or scanner, you can reproduce several charts on a single 8.5- x 11-inch sheet.

A NOTE ON PERSONAL PRONOUNS

To avoid the awkward "he or she" or "his/her" constructions, this book uses the convention of applying feminine pronouns to dealers and masculine pronouns to players. This was an arbitrary choice for convenience of writing and does not carry any implications. Obviously, all dealers are not women and all players are not men.

I. LET IT RIDE

1 – OVERVIEW

Most table games have a history. They have either been around for a long time or they are a modification of another game that has been around for a long time. Let It Ride is different. It was invented by Shuffle Master to help market it's single-deck shuffling machines. Let It Ride was introduced to Nevada casinos in 1993 and quickly became a hit with many table-game players.

Let It Ride is played on a blackjack-like table with, of course, a shuffling machine. It is an unusual type of poker game where you put up all your bets before the first cards are dealt and then you can pull your bets back one-by-one if you don't like the way your hand develops. If you *do* like the cards, you just let your bets ride, as indicated by the name of the game. You can also make an optional side bet to qualify for an additional bonus payout.

The game is easy to learn. Winning hands are based on the standard poker hands, and there are no wild cards. However, unlike blackjack and regular poker, you don't play against the dealer or the other players at the table. Instead, the value of your final hand is determined by a fixed payout schedule. Consequently, the bluffing and normal playing strategies that are used in traditional poker games do not apply.

When the game begins, you put up three equal bets. You can

also place an optional $1 side bet which qualifies you for a separate bonus payout. Three cards are then dealt to each player and two additional community cards are placed in the center of the table. The community cards are exposed one-by-one, becoming a part of each player's hand to eventually form a five-card poker hand. Before the first community card is turned over, you have to decide if your three-card hand is a potential winner or loser. Accordingly, you may either let your first bet ride or pull it back.

The dealer then exposes the first of the two community cards. You now go through the same decision process again and either pull back the second bet or let it ride. Finally, the second community card is turned over so you now have a five-card poker hand. You cannot pull back the third bet—it is kind of a late ante. Also, there are no draws, so the three cards you are dealt plus the two community cards are all you have to work with.

The dealer now evaluates your hand and makes the appropriate payoffs in accordance with the two paytables. To qualify for any kind of a payout, your hand must be at least a pair of tens. If your bets were $5 apiece and you let all of them ride, you could win as much as $15,000 for a royal flush. If you placed the optional side bet, you could win an additional $20,000.

So, isn't Let It Ride simply another version of poker games that use community cards? In a way, but who ever heard of a game in which you put up all your bets before getting a single card and then pull them back one by one? It sounds silly, but the popularity of the game indicates that it works for many people.

In the following chapters, you will learn the rules of play, how special situations are handled, the probabilities of being dealt a winning hand, and the best playing strategy. You will also get information on the basic paytables and the bonus paytables, which can vary from casino to casino. Taking the time to read and learn about these things is one of the best ways to improve your chances of being a winner.

2 – FUNDAMENTALS OF PLAY

THE PLAYING TABLE

Let It Ride is played on a table that is very similar to a blackjack table and is usually located in or near the blackjack area. In most casinos it is easy to find because there is an elevated sign at the table identifying the game. The table has six or seven player positions around the curved side of the table (see Fig. 2). The dealer stands at the flat side with a chip rack directly in front of her and a card-shuffling machine to her right.

At each player position are three betting circles. In most casinos they are marked, from left to right: "$", "2", and "1" (some casinos reverse the order). These circles are where the three mandatory bets are placed prior to dealing a hand. There is also a red-lighted spot above the three betting circles where an optional $1 bonus side bet may be placed. The spot will light up to indicate which players are qualified for the bonus.

Directly in front of the chip rack are two rectangular boxes, sometimes marked with the numbers "1" and "2". This is where the dealer places the two community cards (initially face down).

HOW THE GAME IS PLAYED

The most important goal in Let It Ride is to end up with a five-card poker hand that is at least as good as a pair of tens. For players who invested an extra dollar to qualify for the bonus payout, the secondary goal is to get a hand that is equal or better than the minimum bonus payout. Depending on the particular paytable, this may be a pair of tens, two pairs, or three-of-a-kind.

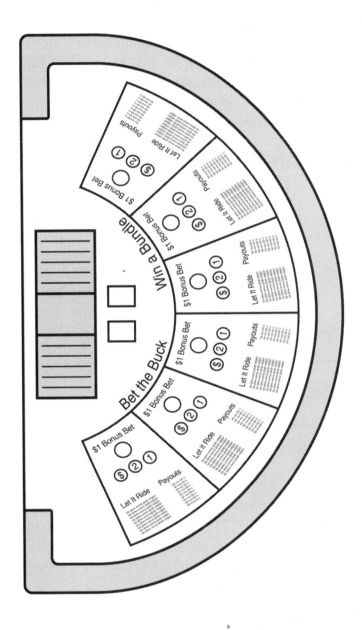

Figure 1 - Typical Let it Ride Table

At the start of each game, you have to place equal bets in each of the three betting circles. Most Let It Ride tables have either a $5 or a $10 minimum bet requirement. This is a little misleading because a $5 minimum means you must bet at least $15 ($5 in each circle). However, if you are unhappy with how your hand develops, you can pull back as much as $10 of your initial $15 bet. When you place your three bets, you may also put a dollar on the red bonus spot. This is entirely optional; however, if you do not invest the dollar, you will have no chance of winning the extra bonus, regardless of how good a hand you might have.

Once all the bets are placed, the dealer distributes three cards face down to each player from a shuffling machine. The dealer also places two cards face down on the two rectangular boxes at the center of the table. These are the two community cards that will ultimately be a part of each player's hand. In some casinos, the community cards are not dealt out until each player has made the first betting decision. You may now look at your three cards, but don't show them to anyone else.

If your hand is a sure winner (has a pair of tens or better), or if you believe the addition of the two community cards will make your hand a winner, you should let the first bet ride. Do this by squaring up the cards and laying them face down directly behind the center bet.

If the hand appears to be a loser, you should lightly scratch the cards on the table (similar to asking for a hit in blackjack). The dealer will then push the first bet out of the circle so that you may retrieve it. Note that pulling back your bet is not the same as folding your hand. You continue to play—you just have less money riding on the hand.

After all the players at the table have made their betting decisions, the dealer turns over the first of the two community cards, and the entire process is repeated. You re-evaluate your hand based on the four cards you now hold. At this time, you can pull back your second bet if the hand does not look good, or "let it ride" if it does. *Keep in mind that you may pull back your second bet even if you let the first bet ride.*

Finally, the dealer turns over the second community card, giving each player the equivalent of five cards. She then proceeds to turn over each player's hand, one by one, and pays off the winners. (The actual payout schedules will be described in the section on payoffs.) Until the dealer turns them over, players are supposed to hide their cards from each other. If you do get a glimpse of another player's hand, it can occasionally help your decision process. How to take advantage of such added information will be covered in the section on playing strategy.

TABLE ETIQUETTE

The first time you ever attended a formal banquet dinner, you were probably intimidated by the number of forks of various shapes and sizes that were sitting to the left of your plate. To avoid embarrassment, the best advice was to carefully watch what the other diners were doing. The same advice applies if you are new to a particular table game. Just watch what the other players are doing and follow their lead. If you do make a mistake, the dealer will correct you. Nowadays most dealers are trained to do this in a polite and unobtrusive way.

The first thing you have to do is to put out three equal bets. Place these bets directly on the three circles in front of you as soon as the dealer has collected all the cards from the previous round. Unless you feel very lucky, follow our strategy advice and bet the table minimum. Although we advise against it, this is also the time to place a $1 bet on the red bonus spot.

After all the cards have been dealt, look at your three cards. Since it is against casino rules to show your cards to anyone else, you should make a reasonable attempt to shield them. Make your betting decision quickly enough so as not to hold up the game. This is easy to do if you remember our strategy rules.

If you decide to "let it ride," square up your cards and place them face down directly behind the center bet. To get your bet back, wait for your turn and then scratch the cards on the felt (like getting a hit in blackjack). Wait for the dealer to push the bet toward you so that you can retrieve it. Once the cards are dealt, you are not allowed to touch any chips on the betting circles.

When the first community card is turned up, the betting decision is repeated. After the second community card is turned up, place your cards face down in front of you. The dealer will then turn over every player's cards, in turn, and make the appropriate pay-offs. Do not toss your cards, but let the dealer turn them over even if you do not have a winning hand.

Tipping, of course, is a matter of personal preference. Instead of tipping a dealer directly, you may prefer to place a bet for the dealer. In this game, placing a bet for the dealer is discouraged because of the multi-tier betting procedure. Most casinos do let you place a dealer bet at the "$" circle. Because the return on this bet is unfavorable, do yourself and the dealer a favor by just tossing her a chip.

3 — THE PAYOFFS
The primary payoffs in Let It Ride are based on a standard paytable that is used by most casinos. Also shown is an alternate paytable that may be used. There are, however, many different bonus paytables for the optional $1 side bet, none of which pay as well as they should. These schedules are all described here.

STANDARD PAYTABLES
After the second community card is exposed, the dealer pays off all the winning hands in accordance with the following paytable.

LET IT RIDE NEVADA PAYTABLE	
HAND	**PAYS**
Royal Flush	1000 to 1
Straight Flush	200 to 1
Four of a Kind	50 to 1
Full House	11 to 1
Flush	8 to 1
Straight	5 to 1
Three of a Kind	3 to 1
Two Pairs	2 to 1
Pair of Tens or better	1 to 1

You don't have to beat anyone to win, neither the dealer nor the other players. If, for example, your final holding is three-of-a-kind and you let all three $5 bets ride, you will be paid $45 ($15 x 3) and get to keep your original bets. If, during the game, you pulled one of your $5 bets back, you will get $30 ($10 x 3) plus your original $10. Should you be fortunate enough to get a royal flush and let all three of your $5 bets ride, you would win $15,000 ($15 x 1000). The payoffs in this game can be very nice.

In some gambling jurisdictions outside of Nevada, the paytable can vary. Following is an example of such an alternate schedule.

LET IT RIDE ALTERNATE PAYTABLE	
HAND	**PAYS**
Royal Flush	500 to 1
Straight Flush	100 to 1
Four of a Kind	25 to 1
Full House	15 to 1
Flush	10 to 1
Straight	5 to 1
Three of a Kind	3 to 1
Two Pairs	2 to 1
Pair of Tens or better	1 to 1

Note that the payoff odds for a full house and flush are higher than in the Nevada paytable. Although this partially compensates for the lower royal flush, straight flush, and four-of-a-kind payoffs, the house edge for this schedule is still about 0.25% higher than for the Nevada paytable.

BONUS PAYOUT SCHEDULES

If you opt to invest an extra dollar on the bonus bet, you will also be qualified for a bonus payoff on certain winning hands. Although almost all casinos offer the bonuses, the paytables are not as standardized as the regular payout schedules. At the present time, there are at least two dozen paytables used in the various gambling jurisdictions around the United States.

Unlike the standard paytables, the payoff odds for the various bonus paytables vary all over the place and the house percentage can range from a low of about 13% to higher than 35%. Consequently, the $1 bonus is not a recommended bet. The most prevalent paytables are shown below, along with the house percentage of each one. The following four paytables are the most common ones found in Nevada, but may also be used elsewhere. As you can see by the outrageous house percentages, investing in this bonus is something we can't recommend.

BONUS PAYTABLE #1 House percentage = 25.5%	
Royal Flush	$20,000
Straight Flush	$2,000
Four of a Kind	$400
Full House	$200
Flush	$50
Straight	$25
Three of a Kind	$5
Two Pairs	No Payout
Pair Tens or better	No Payout

BONUS PAYTABLE #2
House percentage = 25.4%

Royal Flush	$20,000
Straight Flush	$2,000
Four of a Kind	$100
Full House	$75
Flush	$50
Straight	$25
Three of a Kind	$8
Two Pairs	$4
Pair Tens or better	No Payout

BONUS PAYTABLE #3
House percentage = 35.1%

Royal Flush	$20,000
Straight Flush	$2,000
Four of a Kind	$300
Full House	$150
Flush	$50
Straight	$25
Three of a Kind	$5
Two Pairs	No Payout
Pair Tens or better	No Payout

BONUS PAYTABLE
#4 House percentage = 23.7%

Royal Flush	$20,000
Straight Flush	$1,000
Four of a Kind	$100
Full House	$75
Flush	$50
Straight	$25
Three of a Kind	$4
Two Pairs	$3
Pair Tens or better	$1

The New Jersey Casino Control Commission originally approved the following payout schedule. It obviously isn't much better than those used in Nevada. The lack of payouts for tens-or-better and for two pairs means that you won't get a bonus payout very often.

BONUS PAYTABLE #5 House percentage = 24.1%	
Royal Flush	$25,000
Straight Flush	$2,500
Four of a Kind	$400
Full House	$200
Flush	$50
Straight	$25
Three of a Kind	$5
Two Pairs	No Payout
Pair Tens or better	No Payout

Although the following two paytables have a significantly lower house edge, we still can't recommend investing your dollar. Even if you are interested, they are not as easy to find as the horrid tables shown above.

BONUS PAYTABLE #6 House percentage = 13.8%	
Royal Flush	$20,000
Straight Flush	$2,000
Four of a Kind	$100
Full House	$75
Flush	$50
Straight	$25
Three of a Kind	$9
Two Pairs	$6
Pair Tens or better	No Payout

BONUS PAYTABLE #7 House percentage = 13.1%	
Royal Flush	$20,000
Straight Flush	$2,000
Four of a Kind	$200
Full House	$75
Flush	$50
Straight	$25
Three of a Kind	$5
Two Pairs	$4
Pair Tens or better	$1

AGGREGATE PAYOUT LIMIT

Many casinos have a maximum aggregate dollar payout limit on winning hands. This limit is typically $25,000 but, depending on the casino, can range from $10,000 to $100,000. It is actually a deceptive form of betting limit because, while they let you bet as much as you want (up to the table maximum, which can be pretty high), they limit how much they will pay out if you win. The aggregate limit is usually stated on the same little plaque that gives the table betting limits. Or it may be printed on the layout. If you don't see it, ask the dealer.

Ignoring the aggregate limit could cost you a lot of money. Suppose, you are playing at a table with a payout limit of $25,000 and you place three $10 bets as well as a $1 bonus bet. You then let all your bets ride and hit a royal flush. At 1000 to 1 odds (per the standard paytable) you should win $30,000 plus a $20,000 bonus for a total of $50,000; however, the casino will only pay you $25,000. This is clearly a rip-off; but the casinos make the rules and all you can do is avoid falling into the trap. To keep from getting shortchanged on the payoff, never place more than the minimum bet, and don't give them the extra dollar for the bonus bet.

4 — WINNING HANDS

The various card combinations that produce winning hands are the same as in regular poker. Let It Ride uses one standard 52-card deck with no wild cards. The value of a hand depends on which of the following card combinations it contains, listed in order from the highest to the lowest:

Royal Flush:
Five consecutive cards, ten through ace, all of the same suit, as shown below. Simply stated, it is an ace-high straight flush. This is the highest-value hand in Let It Ride. The odds of getting a royal flush are 1 in 649,740 hands.

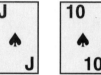

Straight Flush:
Five consecutive cards, all of the same suit, as shown below. The odds of getting a straight flush (excluding a royal flush) are 1 in 72,193 hands.

Four-of-a-Kind:
Four cards of the same rank, as shown below. The fifth card is unrelated to the others. The odds of being dealt four of a kind are 1 in 4,165 hands.

Full House:

Three cards of the same rank and two cards of another rank, that is, three-of-a-kind and a pair. The odds of getting a full house are 1 in 694 hands.

Flush:

Five cards of the same suit, not in sequence, as shown below. The odds of getting a flush are 1 in 509 hands.

Straight:

Five consecutive cards of mixed suits, as shown below. An ace may be either the lowest card as in A-2-3-4-5 or the highest card as in 10-J-Q-K-A. The odds of getting a straight are 1 in 255 hands.

Three-of-a-Kind:

Three cards of the same rank, as shown below. The remaining two cards are unrelated. The odds of getting three of a kind are about 1 in 47 hands.

Two Pairs:

A pair of one rank and a pair of another rank, as shown below. The fifth card is unrelated. The odds of getting two pairs are about 1 in 21 hands.

One Pair:

Two cards of the same rank, as shown below. The three remaining cards are unrelated. The odds of getting any pair are about 1 in 2.4 hands.

The lowest winning hand in Let It Ride is a pair of tens. The odds of getting a pair of tens or any better hand is 1 in 1.63.

5 — PLAYING STRATEGY

Statistically, Let It Ride is a negative expectation game. There is no strategy that will overcome the house edge and make the game profitable for the player. You must, however, use some reasonable strategy when playing this game or you can deplete your bankroll very quickly.

When you play Let It Ride there are four basic decisions you have to make: (1) How much money to wager on the three betting circles, (2) whether or not to place the $1 bonus bet, (3) whether or not to let the first bet ride, and (4) whether or not to let the second bet ride. Each of these four choices will have a major effect on how much you win.

We did try to develop a simplified strategy for Let It Ride, as we did for the other games in this book. Every time we backed off from the best mathematical strategy, however, the house edge just got out of hand. Therefore, we are offering only a single strategy choice for this game, which is a mathematically-perfect strategy. This strategy is not that complex, so even casual recreational players can memorize it easily.

THE PERFECT STRATEGY

There is only one reasonable approach to Let It Ride playing strategy. We call it the *perfect strategy*, and it is outlined in this section. As the name implies, the perfect strategy gets the house take as low as mathematically possible. It is summarized as follows:

PERFECT PLAYING STRATEGY
for Let It Ride

Rule 1: Never bet more than the table minimum.

Rule 2: Never place a $1 bonus bet.

Rule 3: Three-Card Strategy — Let the first bet ride if your initial 3-card hand contains any of the following: Any paying hand (pair of tens or better) A possible royal flush A possible straight flush

Rule 4: Four-Card Strategy — Let the second bet ride if your 4-card hand (including the first community card) contains any of the following: Any paying hand (pair of tens or better) All cards of the same suit An open-ended straight

---

The four rules given for the perfect strategy work very well for most serious and recreational players. It squeezes the last little bit out of the house advantage and may keep you from losing your shirt too quickly. So that you understand them correctly, we will review each of the rules in some detail.

Rule 1.

Since Let It Ride is a negative expectation game, the more you bet, the faster you will drain your resources. The lowest table minimum you are likely to find is $5. Try to play at those tables. If, for instance, you decide to raise your bet to $10, you will actually have to place $30 worth of bets. Also, by placing minimum bets, there is no chance that you will run up against the aggregate payout limit. You wouldn't want to place large bets, get a hot hand, and then get shortchanged on the payout.

Rule 2.

Investing $1 in the bonus bet is a much greater negative expectation gamble than the basic game. In most casinos, the house percentage on the bonus payout ranges from 25 to 35%, or more. Yes, there are schedules that pay the house only 13% or less, but they are very hard to find. Since the house edge on the basic game (with perfect strategy) is as little as 3.5%, why hurt yourself by betting the bonus?

Rule 3. Three-Card Strategy.

Let the first bet ride if your initial 3-card hand contains any paying hand. With three cards the only possible paying hands are three-of-a-kind or a pair of tens or better. If you have one of these winning hands, you don't have to think any further. Just let both bets ride and collect your winnings!

Let the first bet ride if your initial 3-card hand contains a possible royal flush. A possible royal consists of any three cards from a ten to an ace, all of the same suit. Since the payoff for a royal is 1000 to 1, the reason for this rule is obvious.

Let the first bet ride if your initial 3-card hand contains a possible straight flush. This may be either an inside or outside straight flush. If it is inside, however, it should have no more than a one-card gap in the sequence. This hand is worth playing because of the high 200-to-1 payoff; if you miss it, you may still get a flush.

Three-card hands that should not be played: In Let It Ride, there seems to be a tendency for some people to ride out hands on which the bet should be pulled back. Many of them will hopefully play a three-card straight with the odds against completing it being much, much higher (24 to 1) than the meager payoff odds of 5 to 1. Also, never play a pair lower than tens. The chance of picking up a third card of the same rank or making two pairs is worse than the payoff odds of 3 to 1.

Rule 4. Four-Card Strategy.
Let the second bet ride if your 4-card hand contains any paying hand. In addition to three-of-a-kind and a pair of tens or better, a pat four-card hand can also be two pairs or four-of-a-kind. If you have any of these, you know what to do!

Let the second bet ride if your 4-card hand contains all cards of the same suit. In addition to a possible flush, this would include any possible straight flushes.

Let the second bet ride if your 4-card hand contains an open-ended straight. This is a four-card sequence with no gaps, and open at both ends. Thus, the lowest card should not be less than a deuce and the highest card should not be greater than a king.

Four-card hands that should not be played: Some people have a tendency to play inside straights. This is never a good idea. So you started off with a three-card straight flush and the first community card was out-of-suit and turned it into an inside straight. Cut your losses and pull that bet. Or, you were hoping to convert that low pair into a trip. It didn't happen with the first community card, and it probably won't happen with the second one.

PEEKING AT OTHER CARDS
As we have mentioned before, the rule is that you are not supposed to show your cards to any other players. Some people,

however, are sloppy card handlers and it is sometimes easy to get glimpses of other cards. How helpful is this? Sorry to say, but most of the time it is not very worthwhile, and sometimes can lead you into making incorrect strategy decisions.

This is because, although you know the playing strategy, you may not know the basis for it (and we will not go into that, here). For instance, you hold a four-card straight flush and see one of the cards you need in another player's hand. As a result, you decide to pull your second bet. This is a wrong decision! Because of the high 200-to-1 payback, your hand still has a positive expectation of winning. Besides, if you don't make the straight flush, you still have a pretty good chance of getting a flush.

On the other hand, if you are holding a four-card outside straight and see one of the cards you need, the situation is so marginal that how you play it depends on the strength of your straight. If the straight contains a ten or higher, let it ride; if it doesn't, pull the bet. This is because if your straight contains one or more high cards, you also have a chance of hitting a high pair.

We could enumerate a hundred card combinations and the practical effect of seeing additional cards, but the list would be almost impossible to memorize. The bottom line is that, unless you do memorize such a list, your judgement call is as likely to be wrong as it is to be right, so you are better off to just ignore the other player's cards.

CONCLUSION

Let It Ride has two interesting characteristics that sets it apart from the other games in this book. The first is that the players have to put up three equal wagers before the first card is dealt. This does intimidate many beginning players until they get used to the idea. Of course, they can always get back two of those three bets if their hand doesn't develop well.

The second is that the dealer is not an adversary player, but only distributes the cards and makes the payoffs. This seems to have a positive effect on the general attitude at the table. The game is usually pretty relaxed and more sociable than most table games. Furthermore, playing against a fixed payout schedule rather than an unknown quantity (the dealer's hand) seems to reduce over-all tensions.

Even with a house edge of 3.5%, I find the game to be relaxing and rather enjoyable. Of course, I never make the bonus bet.

III. CARIBBEAN STUD POKER

1 – OVERVIEW

As the name implies, Caribbean Stud Poker originated in the Caribbean Islands and on the cruise ships that plied those waters. Because Caribbean Stud was not especially favorable for the player, when Las Vegas casinos adopted the game, they added a progressive jackpot sweetener. Although the jackpot doesn't benefit the player that much, it has helped to make the game popular enough to become a pretty standard offering in Nevada and other gambling jurisdictions.

Caribbean Stud is played on a blackjack-like table. The game is similar to five-card stud poker except that you play against the dealer's hand and not against the other players. You have two opportunities to place a bet on your hand, and you can also make an optional side bet to qualify for the progressive jackpot. If you know a little poker, Caribbean Stud is really quite simple to learn because the winning hands are the same as those in standard poker. However, since you are not competing against the other players at the table, bluffing and other playing strategies that are used in regular stud poker games are of no value.

Just like poker, you start out by putting up an ante. Then the dealer distributes five cards to everyone, including herself. There are no draws, so what you get dealt is what you play. The only decision you have to make is whether or not your hand is likely to beat the dealer. If you think your cards are good enough to win, you may place an additional bet to stay in the running. If you think your hand is a loser, the best move is to fold it and lose your ante.

Should your hand be a winner, and the dealer has a qualifying hand (more on that later), you will be paid in accordance with a basic bonus paytable; the better your hand, the higher the pay-off. You can also go for a second bonus by investing in the optional progressive side bet. Then, if you are fortunate enough to get a royal flush you will win the progressive jackpot. A straight flush wins ten percent of the amount on the progressive meter, while a lesser hand such as four-of-a-kind, a full house, or a flush is paid a fixed bonus, ranging from $50 to $500. As you can see, Caribbean Stud is a game based on bonus payouts. In fact, the two chances of collecting a bonus payment for each hand are the major attraction for most players.

In the following sections, you will learn the rules of play, how special situations are handled, the probabilities of being dealt a winning hand, and the best playing strategy. You will also get information on the basic bonus paytables and the progressive bonus paytables, which can vary from casino to casino. Taking the time to read and learn about these things is one of the best ways to improve your chances of being a winner.

2 – FUNDAMENTALS OF PLAY

THE PLAYING TABLE
Caribbean Stud is played on a table that is very similar to a blackjack table and is usually located in or near the blackjack area. In most casinos it is easy to find because there is an elevated sign at the table identifying the game. The table has six or seven player

positions around the curved side of the table (see Fig. 1). The dealer stands at the flat side with a chip rack directly in front of her and a shuffling machine to her right. A Shuffle Master shuffling machine is used by most casinos. It shuffles a single 52-card deck each time a new hand is dealt.

At each player position are two betting spots and a slot. The spot nearest the dealer, marked ANTE, is where the initial bets are placed. The other spot is marked BET. That is where you should put the second bet if, after viewing your dealt hand, you decide to continue playing. If you wish to participate in the progressive jackpot, you may place a $1 chip in the progressive slot located above the two betting spots.

HOW THE GAME IS PLAYED

The initial goal in Caribbean Stud is to get a better five-card poker hand than the dealer has. If that goal is met, and the dealer has a *qualifying* hand, the next goal is to get a strong enough hand to pay a basic bonus that is better than even money. To be qualified, a dealer's hand must contain at least an ace and a king; this is explained more fully in the next section. If you invest a dollar in the progressive jackpot, the final goal is to get a flush or better hand, which will earn a progressive bonus payout. Or, better yet, to get a royal flush and win the entire progressive jackpot pool.

The game begins when everyone places their initial bets in the ANTE box. Most Caribbean Stud games have either a $5 or a $10 minimum bet requirement. At this time, you may also place a dollar chip or coin in the progressive slot. This is entirely optional; however, if you do not invest the dollar, you will have no chance of winning a progressive bonus or the progressive jackpot. When all the bets have been placed, the dealer pushes a button causing the progressive bets to drop into a collection box. You'll then see a red light go on in front of those players who

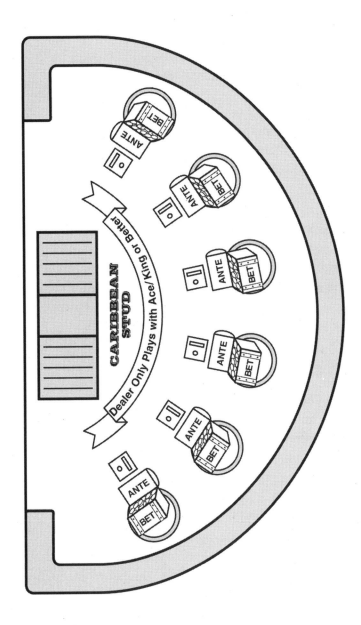

Figure 2 - Typical Caribbean Stud Table

made the $1 bet and qualify for the progressive jackpot and bonuses. The ante bets stay in place on the table.

The dealer distributes five cards face down to each player. She also deals herself five cards face down and then turns one of her cards face up. The cards are almost always dealt from a shuffling machine. Since you now have to make a strategy decision on the strength of your hand, the dealer's upcard is supposed to give you a clue as to how to proceed. Contrary to blackjack, this upcard is not much help.

You now have to decide if your hand is good enough to invest more money. This is the call or fold decision. If you believe your hand may beat the dealer, you can call (stay in the game) by placing an additional wager. This call bet is put in the BET box and must be exactly double the original ante. That is, if the ante was $5, then the additional bet must be $10, for a total investment of $15. After the call bet is placed, lay your cards face down to the left of the BET box. If you think your hand is not good enough to beat the dealer, you can avoid risking more money by folding your hand. This action forfeits the ante as well as the $1 progressive bet (if it was made).

The players are supposed to hide their cards from each other until the dealer turns them over to determine the payoffs. This is simply an example of casino paranoia, because if you do get a glimpse of another player's hand, it won't be of much help in making the call-or-fold decision. I'll give you more details on this in the section on playing strategy.

After all the players have decided whether to call or fold, the dealer turns over her four downcards for everyone to see. If the dealer's hand is qualified, the active player's hands (those who didn't fold) are turned over one by one and the appropriate payoffs are made. The amounts of the payoffs are based on the basic bonus paytable and also depend on whether or not the dealer has a qualifying hand. In addition, those players who made the optional $1 progressive bet (and didn't fold), are paid in accordance with the progressive bonus paytable. The progressive payoff is not affected by the qualification status of the dealer's hand.

If the dealer's hand is not qualified and you made the call bet, you automatically win your ante bet at even money, and your call bet is returned. No basic bonuses are paid; however, if you made the $1 progressive bet you will still be paid according to that paytable.

THE QUALIFYING HAND

As we already mentioned, to be qualified, the dealer's hand must contain at least an ace and a king. Consequently, any pair or higher is also qualified, as well as straights, flushes, and straight flushes. The lowest qualified hand is A-K-4-3-2, as shown below, which could be beat by a player holding A-K-5-3-2 or better.

The highest *non*-qualifying hand is A-Q-J-10-9, as shown below. By the rules of poker, this is a lower hand than the minimum qualifying hand, because the second-highest card is a queen instead of a king.

When the dealer has a qualifying hand, the game proceeds in a normal manner. That is, you have to beat the dealer's hand to win. When the dealer's hand is not qualified, the dealer folds and there is no competitive play. Regardless of how good a hand you hold, you only win the ante bet at even money. In either case, if you made the $1 progressive bet *and didn't fold your hand,* you are paid according to the progressive jackpot and bonus paytable.

TABLE ETIQUETTE

As we have said before, if you are new to a game just watch what the other players are doing and try to do the same. If you make a mistake in table protocol, the dealer will politely correct you.

The first thing you have to do is put out your ante wager. Place the bet directly on the ANTE box as soon as the dealer has collected all the cards from the previous round. Unless you feel very lucky, follow our strategy advice and bet the table minimum. Although we advise against it, this is also the time to place a $1 coin in the progressive slot.

After all the cards have been dealt, look at your five cards. Since it is against casino rules to show your cards to anyone else, you should make a reasonable attempt to shield them. Make your bet-or-fold decision quickly enough so as not to hold up the game. This is easy to do if you remember our strategy rules.

If you decide to fold, toss your cards (face down) toward the dealer. She will place them in the discard stack and remove your ante. If you decide to bet, place double the amount of your ante on the BET box and lay your cards face down next to the bet. Never touch your original ante wager. Now you are done, and the dealer takes over.

If the dealer's hand qualifies, the dealer will turn over each active player's cards, in turn, and make the appropriate payoffs.

Should the dealer not qualify, she will simply collect the cards and pay the antes.

Important note: If you made the $1 progressive bet and your hand qualifies for a progressive bonus, you must be alert because some non-qualifying dealers may neglect to check your cards. To avoid being shortchanged, you must be ready to tell the dealer that you are a winner. Once your cards hit the discard stack, it is too late to prove that you won a bonus.

Tipping, of course, is a matter of personal preference. Instead of tipping a dealer directly, you may prefer to place a bet for the dealer. In Caribbean Stud, placing a bet for the dealer is discouraged because of the two-tier betting procedure. If you want to tip the dealer, it is simpler to just toss her a chip.

3 – THE PAYOFFS

THE BASIC BONUS
As we said earlier, how the payoffs in Caribbean Stud are handled depends on whether or not the dealer has a qualifying hand. When the dealer's hand is qualified, your hand is pitted against the dealer's. If you win, you are paid in accordance with the basic bonus schedule. When the dealer's hand is not qualified, the dealer has effectively dropped out of the game and you are an automatic winner (if you didn't fold). However, you only win even money on the ante bet, and the basic bonus paytable does not pay off.

DEALER'S HAND IS QUALIFIED
When the dealer's hand is qualified, your hand is compared against the dealer's. If the dealer's hand beats or ties your hand, you lose both the ante and the call bet. If your hand *beats* the dealer's hand, you win both bets.

The ante bet gets paid even money and the call bet gets paid in accordance with the following paytable:

BASIC BONUS PAYTABLE	
HAND	**PAYS**
Royal Flush	100 to 1
Straight Flush	50 to 1
Four of a Kind	20 to 1
Full House	7 to 1
Flush	5 to 1
Straight	4 to 1
Three of a Kind	3 to 1
Two Pairs	2 to 1
One Pair or less	1 to 1

For example: Assume you start off with a $5 ante bet and are dealt three sevens plus two odd cards, as in the following hand:

This looks like a good hand, so you stay in the game by placing a $10 call bet, which, according to the rules, is double the ante bet. The dealer turns over her cards and shows a pair of nines, which is a qualified hand.

Since your three sevens beat the dealer's hand, you are paid $5 (even money) for the ante and $30 (3 to 1 odds) for the call bet, winning a total of $35. You, of course, also get back your original investment of $15.

DEALER'S HAND IS NOT QUALIFIED

When the dealer's hand does not contain at least an ace-king, you automatically win the ante bet (at even money), even if your hand is not as good as the dealer's. The call bet, however, becomes a push. That is, the call bet is returned to you with no additional payoff.

For example, assume, as before, that you start off with a $5 ante bet and are dealt three sevens plus two odd cards, so you stay in the game by placing a $10 call bet. The dealer turns over her cards and shows an ace, a jack, and three small odd cards, which is not a qualified hand.

You are only paid $5 (even money) for the ante and get nothing for the call bet of $10. So you win a total of $5 and also get back your original investment of $15.

This is the biggest disappointment in the game of Caribbean Stud, especially if you have a good hand. It basically means that if the dealer's hand is very weak, the casino gets off the hook by only paying off the ante bet—a very small penalty. This is the major failing of Caribbean Stud and has caused many players to gravitate to more pleasant games.

BASIC BONUS PAYOUT LIMIT

All casinos have a maximum dollar payout limit for the basic bonus. Depending on the casino, the limit can range from $5,000 to $50,000. This is actually a deceptive form of betting limit. We call it deceptive because, while they let you bet as much as you want (up to the table maximum, which can be pretty high), they limit how much they will pay out if you win.

The aggregate limit is usually stated on the same plaque that gives the table betting limits. If you don't see it, ask the dealer.

Suppose, with a payout limit of $5,000, you make a $100 call bet and hit a royal flush. At 100 to 1 odds (per the basic bonus paytable) you should win $10,000; however, the casino will only pay you $5,000. What a bummer! To avoid getting shortchanged on the payoff, never place a call bet that is more than one hundredth of the payout limit. For example, if the payout limit is $5,000, divide that number by 100 and keep your call bet to less than $50. Since the call bet is always twice the ante, the ante bet in this example should not exceed $25.

One bright note is that the payout limit only applies to the basic bonus. The progressive bonus (see below) does not have a limit because it pays predetermined dollar amounts.

THE PROGRESSIVE BONUS

The good news is that the progressive bonus pays off whether or not the dealer's hand is qualified, so long as you placed $1 in the progressive slot at the start of the hand and you stayed in the hand by placing the call bet. Furthermore, you get paid *even if the dealer has a better hand*. This sounds marvelous, but it is only good for liberal payoff schedules and when the progressive meter gets quite high, as we will see in the strategy section.

The Progressive Jackpot Meter that is located at the Caribbean Stud table is usually linked to all the Caribbean Stud games in that casino. Every time a player pays in a dollar, the meter goes a little bit higher. How fast it rises depends on how much of that dollar is added to the jackpot pool, and this depends on the particular casino. Some casinos put in as much as 75 cents, while the greedier ones may put in only about 50 cents out of every dollar collected.

In all casinos, a royal flush wins the entire progressive jackpot and a straight flush wins ten% of the amount on the progressive meter. A four of a kind, a full house, or a flush will win a fixed dollar amount as defined on the progressive bonus paytable. The exact amount of these fixed bonuses varies from casino to casino. The following paytable is one example of what you will find in some casinos:

PROGRESSIVE BONUS PAYTABLE	
HAND	**PAYS**
Royal Flush	Full Jackpot
Straight Flush	10% of Jackpot
Four of a Kind	$250
Full House	$100
Flush	$50

The above table is not typical, however, because there are too many different paytables for any one of them to be typical. In a few casinos, four of a kind might pay as much as $500, a full house can pay up to $250, and a flush can pay $100. If you want to invest in the progressive jackpot, you should search for the best payouts. Not only is the level of the progressive meter important, but the amount of the fixed payoffs can have a significant effect on the overall payback of the game. More specific information on these paytables is given in the strategy section.

Finally, the progressive payouts for a royal flush and a straight flush are considered to be aggregate. That means if two players got royal flushes on the same deal, they would split the progressive jackpot. The same applies to a straight flush. Two players with straight flushes would split the 10% jackpot, thus getting 5% apiece. You really don't need to worry about this because the appearance of two straight flushes or two royal flushes in the same deal has never occurred. The aggregate rule only applies to the royal flush and the straight flush.

The other hands listed on the progressive bonus paytable are always paid the full amount shown.

4 – WINNING HANDS

The various card combinations that produce winning hands are the same as in regular poker. Caribbean Stud uses one 52-card deck with no wild cards. Suits have no relative value; they only come into play for a flush, a straight flush, or a royal flush. The value of a hand depends on which of the following card combinations it contains, listed in order from the highest to the lowest:

Royal Flush:
An ace-high straight flush, as shown below, is the highest-value hand in Caribbean Stud. The odds of being dealt a royal flush are 1 in 649,740 hands.

Since suits do not have any relative value, two royal flushes of different suits constitute a tie. Since there is no record of this event ever having occurred, we are not going to worry about it.

Straight Flush:
Five consecutive cards, all of the same suit, as shown below. The odds of being dealt a straight flush (excluding a royal flush) are 1 in 72,193 hands.

Should the dealer and a player both have straight flushes, the hand containing the highest-ranking card is the winner. A king-high is the best straight flush; the hand shown above is a jack-high straight flush. If both the dealer and player have identical straight flushes (except for the suit), then the dealer wins. The player will still win ten% of the progressive jackpot if the side bet was made. Should two players have straight flushes, and both made the side bet, then the ten-percent jackpot is split.

Four-of-a-Kind:
Four cards of the same rank, as shown below. The fifth card is unrelated to the others. The odds of being dealt four of a kind are 1 in 4,165 hands.

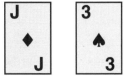

Should the dealer and a player both have four of a kind, the one with the highest rank is the winner.

Full House:
Three cards of the same rank and two cards of another rank, that is, three-of-a-kind and a pair. The odds of being dealt a full house are 1 in 694 hands.

Should the dealer and a player both have a full house, the hand with the highest ranked three of a kind is the winner. The ranks of the pairs are immaterial.

Flush:

Five cards of the same suit, not in sequence, as shown below. The odds of being dealt a flush are 1 in 509 hands.

Should the dealer and a player both have flushes, the one containing the highest ranked card is the winner. If the highest ranked card in both hands is the same, then the second-highest ranked card is the tiebreaker. If that is also the same, then the third-, the fourth-, and the fifth-highest cards are compared. If all five cards in both hands are the same rank, the dealer wins.

Straight:

Five consecutive cards of mixed suits, as shown below. An ace may be either the lowest card as in A-2-3-4-5 or the highest card as in 10-J-Q-K-A. The odds of being dealt a straight are 1 in 255 hands.

Should the dealer and a player both have straights, the one containing the highest ranked card is the winner. If the highest ranked card in both hands is the same, the dealer wins.

Three-of-a-Kind:

Three cards of the same rank, as shown below. The remaining two cards are unrelated. The odds of being dealt three of a kind are about 1 in 47 hands.

Should the dealer and a player both have three of a kind, the one with the highest rank is the winner.

Two Pairs:

A pair of one rank and a pair of another rank, as shown below. The fifth card is unrelated. The odds of being dealt two pairs are about 1 in 21 hands.

Should the dealer and a player both have two pairs, the one with the highest-ranked pair is the winner. If the highest-ranked pair in both hands is the same, then the one having the highest-ranked second pair wins. If both pairs are the same rank, then the hand with the highest fifth card wins. If all cards are the same rank, the dealer wins.

One Pair:

Two cards of the same rank. The three remaining cards are unrelated. The odds of being dealt a pair are about 1 in 2.4 hands.

The highest-ranked pair wins. If two hands contain pairs of the same rank, then the one with the highest-ranked odd card wins. If that card is the same, then the fourth and fifth cards break the tie in the hands. If all cards are the same rank, the dealer wins.

Ace-King:

A hand that contains none of the above poker hands, but does have one ace and one king, as shown below. The three remaining cards are unrelated. The odds of being dealt exactly one ace and one king (plus three mixed cards) are about 1 in 15 hands.

For the dealer, this is the lowest value qualifying hand. If a player also has an ace-king hand, then the hand with the highest ranked of the remaining three cards wins. If all cards are the same rank, the dealer wins. The odds of being dealt an ace-king hand *or better* are about 1 in 1.8. The odds of being dealt an ace-king hand *or less* are 1 in 2. As we shall see in the next section, these odds are important because this is the pivotal hand for determining the best playing strategy.

Low Cards:

A hand that contains none of the above poker hands, but has mixed cards no higher than one ace and one queen, as shown below. The odds of being dealt an ace-queen hand or lower are about 1 in 2.3 hands.

This is a non-qualifying hand for the dealer. For the player, the hand has no value and should never be called.

5 — PLAYING STRATEGY

From a statistical standpoint, Caribbean Stud is a negative expectation game. Unlike blackjack, there is no strategy that will overcome the house edge and make the game profitable for the player. Sure, you can simply wait until the progressive meter gets high enough to nullify the house take, but that does not happen very often. In most casinos, the jackpot will have to exceed a half million dollars for the overall player expectation to become positive. So far this has never happened, but when and if it does, you will find it very difficult to get a seat at the table.

You must still use some reasonable strategy when playing this game or you will deplete your bankroll very quickly. The Caribbean Stud player has three basic decisions to make: (1) How much money to ante, (2) whether or not to place the $1 progressive bet, and (3) whether to place the call bet (which has to be double the ante) or fold the hand and lose the ante. Each of these three choices will have a major effect on how fast you will lose your money.

A SIMPLE STRATEGY

We developed two approaches to Caribbean Stud playing strategy, one for recreational players and one for serious players. The first is a *simple strategy*, which is outlined in this section, and the second is a *perfect strategy*, which is explained and described in the next section. As the name implies, the simple strategy is very elementary.

It is summarized on the following page:

SIMPLE PLAYING STRATEGY
for Caribbean Stud Poker

Rule 1: Never ante more than the table minimum.
Rule 2: Never bet on the progressive jackpot.
Rule 3: Call if hand contains an Ace-King-Queen or better.
Otherwise, fold.

That's all there is to it. Yes, these strategy rules are oversimplified, but they may keep you from losing your shirt. Just so you know that they are valid, we will analyze each one of the rules.

Rule 1.

Since Caribbean Stud is a negative expectation game, the more you bet, the faster you will lose. The lowest table minimum you are likely to find is $5. Try to play at those tables. If, for instance, you decide to wager $10 on your ante, the call bet has to be $20. When you follow the simple strategy, you will call about every other hand. On folded hands you will invest (and lose) $10, and on the called hands you will invest $30 ($10 ante plus $20 call)—which averages out to a risk of $20 per hand. If you are going to play at that level or higher, you should take the time to read the rest of this section and learn the perfect strategy.

Rule 2.

Even disregarding the house edge, 95% of the time, investing $1 in the progressive jackpot is a negative expectation gamble. In many casinos, the jackpot would have to exceed $200,000 for the expectation to go positive. If you really want to go for the gold, do me a favor and read the rest of the chapter.

Rule 3.

This is a simplification of the perfect strategy. It means that you should call when you have any pair or better, as well as an ace-king hand when the third-highest card is a queen. There is some benefit to playing other ace-king hands, but you have to learn more complicated rules, and the advantage is very small. If you misapply the other rules, you may be worse off than if you just stick to the ace-king-queen rule. That's why we call it a simple strategy.

If you don't like things to get too complicated, you can stop reading right here, because these three simple rules will carry you a long way. Those of you who are ready to learn the fine points of Caribbean Stud strategy have to read the rest of the chapter.

THE PERFECT STRATEGY

Although the three rules given for the simple strategy work very well for most recreational players, some folks are willing to exert that extra effort needed to squeeze the last little bit out of the house advantage. If that's what you want to do, we will show you how. The perfect strategy that we recommend is as follows:

PERFECT PLAYING STRATEGY
for Caribbean Stud Poker

Rule 1: Never ante more than the table minimum.

Rule 2: Bet $1 on progressive jackpot only when the meter exceeds the positive expectation breakpoint.

Rule 3: Call if hand contains an **Ace-King-Jack-9-5** or better. Otherwise, fold.

Rule 4: Ignore the dealer's upcard.

Before continuing, it should be mentioned that no two books on Caribbean Stud are in complete agreement as to the best playing strategy. We don't know exactly why, because we don't have access to anyone else's detailed calculations or simulation code. Understandably, the math is a bit tricky and it is easy to make errors in designing a simulation program. Our perfect strategy, which is based on mathematical analyses, is somewhat different than strategies published by others, but we believe the calculations to be correct and will stand by them.

THE ANTE

The best approach in Caribbean Stud is to risk as little money as possible. Try to find a $5 table and only place the minimum bet. This is the same rule as for the simple strategy. There is more than one reason for this strong recommendation. Being a negative expectation game, the heavier you bet, the more you will lose (barring a lucky streak). If that doesn't convince you, there is a second reason.

The big draw for most people that play Caribbean Stud is the progressive jackpot. And we agree that when the jackpot gets into the hundreds of thousands of dollars, that is a good time to invest in the $1 progressive bet. There is, however, an important point to keep in mind: *The progressive bonus and jackpot payoffs are exactly the same whether you placed a $5 ante or a $25 ante.* Why risk more money than you need to when the chance of making a good hand and the payoff for that hand have no bearing on the amount that you bet.

You also have to keep in mind when you ante, that you can't win anything unless you also place the call bet. That means a $5 ante turns into a $15 investment and a $25 ante turns into a $75 investment—*per hand.* As you will see in the following section, you will fold your hand about half of the time. And each time you fold, you will lose your ante. It is better to lose $5 than to lose $25.

Finally, by placing a minimum ante bet, there is no chance that you will run up against the bonus payout limit. You wouldn't want to place a large bet, get a hot hand, and then get short-changed on the payout. That would be a cruel blow.

TO CALL OR TO FOLD

The basic decision in Caribbean Stud is whether to call or to fold. In the simple strategy we boiled it down to whether or not you have at least an ace-king-queen. To squeeze the most out of the mathematical probabilities, there are other ace-king hands that should also be played. We will now look at these and other hands one-by-one.

One pair or better.

All hands that contain at least one pair are potential winners and should always be called. Hands that contain two pairs or better are quite strong. If the dealer has a qualifying hand, such strong hands will win the basic bonus most of the time. A pair of sevens or better will beat the dealer's hand most of the time.

The actual break point between a positive and negative expectation is a pair of sixes. Specifically, a pair of sixes with a Q-8-7 or better is, on average, a positive expectation hand. Why then, should you ever call a hand with less than a pair of sixes? Because, although you will, on average, lose some money, you will lose less than if you fold your hand and give up the ante. In other words, you are limiting your losses.

Ace-King hand.

Since Caribbean Stud is a negative expectation game, limiting your losses is really the main strategy. Whenever you hold an ace-king hand, that is exactly what you are doing. To minimize your losses, the strategy advises that you should hold any hand that, in the long run, is likely to lose less than the amount of a forfeited ante.

The poorest hand for which the expected long-term loss is less than the amount of the ante is an ace-king with a jack-9-5, as shown here.

This hand is the strategy breakpoint. You should call any hand that is an A-K-J-9-5 or better and you should fold any hand that is an A-K-J-9-4 or worse.

In the simple strategy, the lowest suggested call hand is an A-K-Q. The reason for this is that the difference in the expected payback between an A-K-Q hand and an A-K-J-9-5 hand is very minimal, and A-K-Q is much easier to remember. However, if you want to squeeze out that extra tenth of a%, use the A-K-J-9-5 as your call/fold breakpoint.

THE DEALER'S UPCARD

Our calculations show that the dealer's upcard has little, if any, strategic value to the player and, therefore, should be ignored. Since this is contrary to most published strategies, we will try to explain our rationale in non-mathematical terms.

The advice given in most books is that if the rank of one of your five cards matches the rank of the dealer's upcard, you should call your hand if it contains an ace-king or better. The explanation usually given is that the dealer's upcard is less apt to be paired or tripled if one of the remaining three cards of that rank is in the player's hand. In other words, the dealer has one less chance of having a pair, three-of-a-kind, or full house, and has no chance of having four-of-a-kind with that upcard.

We disagree with this strategy and believe that calling all ace-king hands when the upcard is matched will result in higher losses than necessary, for the following reasons:

1. Aside from the dealer's hand, there are 47 outstanding cards. These are the cards in all the players hands plus the remaining cards in the deck. Unless the dealer already has four-of-a-kind, one or more of these outstanding 47 cards *must* match the dealer's upcard. Therefore, the fact that one of the matching cards happens to be in your hand is statistically immaterial, and the chances of the dealer qualifying or getting certain winning hands is relatively unchanged.

2. The advice to bet on all ace-king hands with a matching upcard will result in more losses than wins, especially since the call bet has to be *double* the ante. The lowest value ace-king hand is A-K-4-3-2, which can't beat any qualified dealer hand. The only way it can win anything is if the dealer does not qualify, and that happens only 43.7% of the time. A slightly better hand such as A-K-5-3-2 or A-K-6-3-2 will be beat by a qualified hand 99.4% of the time. The theory is that these hands will win more often because the dealer is less apt to be qualified.

To overcome call bet losses, however, the percentage of non-qualified hands would have to increase from 43.7 to 75%. Matching one of the dealer's cards is not going to do that. No, this is not the way to survive in Caribbean Stud.

One final note about seeing other cards. In Caribbean Stud, you are supposed to hide your cards from the other players—presumably to keep you from getting extra help on how to play your hand. In regular poker, getting a glimpse of another player's hand can be a major clue in determining how to bet. Theoretically, this is also an advantage in Caribbean Stud except that the probability calculations are too complex to perform without a computer. Thus, from a practical standpoint, seeing a hand (other than the dealer's) is of little or no value.

THE PROGRESSIVE JACKPOT

One of the lures in Caribbean Stud is the possibility of getting a royal flush and winning the progressive jackpot, or winning lesser amounts for certain other hands. Entering the progressive jackpot pool is entirely optional; however, if you do not put up the dollar, you will have no chance of winning the progressive jackpot or one of the progressive bonuses.

The progressive bonuses and the progressive jackpot pay off whether or not the dealer's hand is qualified, so long as you placed $1 in the progressive slot at the start of the hand and you don't fold. If your hand is a flush, full house, or four-of-a-kind, you get paid a progressive bonus even if the dealer has a better hand. The same is true for a royal flush or straight flush.

Investing in the progressive pool is only worthwhile when the progressive meter gets quite high. Following are examples of paytables showing the minimum jackpot needed for a positive expectation of winning. This positive expectation only applies to the progressive bonus or jackpot, not to the entire game.

To overcome the house edge on the basic game, the progressive jackpot would have to reach levels that have never before been attained.

The four paytables shown on the following pages are representative examples of the many different schedules you will find in various casinos and various gaming jurisdictions. They represent the worst to the best plus a couple of in-between examples.

PROGRESSIVE BONUS PAYTABLE #1

HAND	PAYS
Royal Flush	Full Jackpot
Straight Flush	10% of Jackpot
Four of a Kind	$100
Full House	$75
Flush	$50

For this schedule, place $1 progressive bet only if jackpot exceeds $264,000.

PROGRESSIVE BONUS PAYTABLE #2

HAND	PAYS
Royal Flush	Full Jackpot
Straight Flush	10% of Jackpot
Four of a Kind	$250
Full House	$125
Flush	$75

For this schedule, place $1 progressive bet only if jackpot exceeds $210,000.

PROGRESSIVE BONUS PAYTABLE #3

HAND	PAYS
Royal Flush	Full Jackpot
Straight Flush	10% of Jackpot
Four of a Kind	$500
Full House	$150
Flush	$75

For this schedule, place $1 progressive bet only if jackpot exceeds $177,000.

PROGRESSIVE BONUS PAYTABLE #4

HAND	PAYS
Royal Flush	Full Jackpot
Straight Flush	10% of Jackpot
Four of a Kind	$500
Full House	$250
Flush	$100

For this schedule, place $1 progressive bet only if jackpot exceeds $111,000.

Progressive paytables #1 and #2 are quite prevalent, especially in Nevada. You shouldn't waste your progressive dollar on these unless the meter is well over $200,000, which is a rare occurrence. Paytable #3 is somewhat better and is worth the risk if the meter is over $170,000. However, it will take a while to get there, since the meter is reset to $50,000 whenever the jackpot is paid out. Paytable #4 is as good as it gets. It may be found in some of the newer casinos that are trying to boost player interest in the game. In this schedule, the break point of $111,000 may actually be reached once in a while.

When you find a paytable that falls in-between two of the above, you should either estimate the jackpot break point or use the higher one as your guide. Keep in mind that the calculations for the above amounts were based on a $1 bet. If you encounter a table where the progressive bet is $2, the positive expectation break points range from $453,000 to $605,000. Since no Caribbean Stud progressive meter has ever gotten that high, playing the progressive at such a table is not advisable.

One last point: Every book on Caribbean Stud gives a different break-even amount for the progressive bonus. We find this to be puzzling, since the mathematics is pretty straightforward. In any case, we stand by our numbers.

CONCLUSION

Caribbean Stud is an enigma. It is an unsatisfying and sometimes annoying game with an excessive house edge of 5.3% and a progressive jackpot that seldom gets high enough to be worth playing, yet it maintains its popularity. A lot of people seem to enjoy playing it, but I feel differently. After losing a few hands and finally getting a triplet or a straight that should pay a nice 4 to 1 or 5 to 1, it is maddening when the dealer gets off the hook by not qualifying. I can only take so much of that.

While watching the game, I have rarely seen a player who does not invest a dollar in the progressive, especially when the progressive meter exceeds $100,000. Of course, they haven't a clue as to where the expectation breakpoint might be. For many people, risking one dollar on the chance of winning $100,000 or more is too much to resist, even if they know the positive expectation breakpoint is over $200,000. That is also why so many people play the state lotteries.

IV. THREE CARD POKER

1 — OVERVIEW

Three Card Poker is a variation of an English game known as Brag. The American version was invented and introduced by Prime Table Games under the nondescript name of Brit-Brag. It was renamed Three Card Poker and is currently being distributed by Shuffle Master. It is a fast-moving game that combines some of the better attributes of Caribbean Stud and Let It Ride. As a result, it is rapidly becoming a mainstay in many casinos, especially in Mississippi where there are more Three Card Poker tables than on the Las Vegas Strip.

Like the other games in this book, Three Card Poker is played on a blackjack-like table. The game is similar to five-card stud poker except that you get only three cards and play against the dealer's hand and not against the other players. You have two opportunities to place a direct wager on your hand. In addition, you can make an independent side bet to qualify for a bonus payout.

The game is easy to learn and the playing strategy is very simple. Within the three-card constraint, winning hands are based on a variation of standard poker hands. There are no wild cards. Because, like blackjack, you play against the dealer rather than against the other players at the table, the bluffing and normal playing strategies that are used in regular poker games do not apply.

When the game begins, you may put up an initial ante wager and/or place a side bet in the Pair Plus circle. The dealer then distributes three cards to each player and to herself. There are no draws or community cards, so the three-card hand you are dealt is all you have to work with. The only decision you have to make is whether or not your hand is likely to beat the dealer. If you think your cards are good enough to win, you may place an additional wager to stay in the running. If you think your hand is a loser, the best move is to fold your hand and lose the ante.

Should your hand be a winner, and the dealer has a qualifying hand (more on that later), you will be paid even money. If you have a straight or better, you will also collect a bonus. If you placed the independent Pair Plus side bet, you will win a bonus for a pair or better, regardless of whether or not you beat the dealer. These bonus payouts add interest and appeal to the game.

In the following sections, you will learn the rules of play, how special situations are handled, the probabilities of being dealt a winning hand, and the best playing strategy. You will also get information on the ante bonus and the Pair Plus bonus payouts. Learning about these things before you sit down at a Three card Poker table will improve your chances of being a winner.

2 — FUNDAMENTALS OF PLAY

THE PLAYING TABLE
Three Card Poker is played on a table that is similar to a black-jack table and is usually located in or near the blackjack area. In most casinos it is easy to find because there is an elevated sign at the table identifying the game. The table has six or seven player positions around the curved side of the table (see Fig. 5). The dealer stands at the flat side with a chip rack directly in front of her and a card-shuffling machine to her right.

At each player position are three betting spaces. The circle nearest the dealer, marked PAIR PLUS, is where the bonus side bet may be placed. The center space, marked ANTE, is where your initial bet should be placed. The third space, nearest the player, is marked PLAY. That is where to put the second bet if, after viewing your dealt hand, you decide to continue playing.

HOW THE GAME IS PLAYED

The initial goal in Three Card Poker is to get a better three-card poker hand than the dealer's. If that goal is met, and the dealer has a qualifying hand, the next goal is to get a strong enough hand to pay an ante bonus. So long as you didn't fold, the ante bonus pays off for a straight, a straight flush, or three-of-a-kind, regardless of whether you beat the dealer or the dealer is qualified.

To be *qualified*, a dealer's hand must contain at least a queen. We explain this more fully in the next section. If you placed an optional bet on the PAIR PLUS circle, the final goal is to get a pair or better to win a Pair Plus bonus. This bonus pays off independently of the rest of the game.

At the beginning of each hand, you have to place a wager in the ANTE box, or a wager in the PAIR PLUS circle, or both. You have the option of not putting up an ante and only betting the Pair Plus, but then you are playing against the Pair Plus bonus schedule rather than against the dealer. When everyone has placed their ante and/or Pair Plus bets, the dealer distributes three cards face down to each player and to herself. The cards are usually dealt from a shuffling machine that uses a single 52-card deck with no wild cards.

You now have to decide if your hand is good enough to invest more money. If you believe your hand may beat the dealer, you can stay in the game by placing an additional wager. This call bet is put in the PLAY box and must be exactly the same amount as the original ante. That is, if the ante was $10, then the additional wager must also be $10, for a total investment of $20. If you feel that your hand is not good enough to beat the dealer, you can fold and lose the ante. This is done by laying the cards face-down and not placing a play bet. The dealer will then remove your cards and your ante.

Until the dealer turns them over to determine the payoff, you are supposed to hide your cards from the other players. If you do get a glimpse of another player's hand, it could help in making the bet-or-fold decision. We will cover this in the section on playing strategy.

After all the players have decided whether to bet or fold, the dealer turns over her cards for everyone to see. If the dealer's hand is qualified, the active player's hands (those that didn't fold) are turned over one by one and the appropriate payoffs are made. The amounts of the payoffs are based on the ante bonus paytable and also depend on whether or not the dealer has a qualifying hand. In addition, if you made a Pair Plus bet, you will be paid in accordance with the Pair Plus paytable. The Pair Plus payout is not affected by the qualification status of the dealer's hand.

If the dealer's hand is not qualified and you did not fold your hand, you automatically win your ante bet at even money and get back your play bet. In addition, both the ante bonus and the Pair Plus bonus are paid according to the respective paytables.

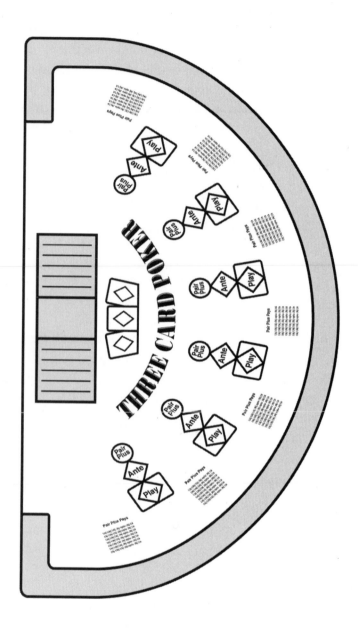

Figure 3 - Typical Three Card Poker Table

THE QUALIFYING HAND

To be qualified, the dealer's hand must contain at least a queen. On average, the dealer is dealt a qualifying hand about 44% of the time. The lowest qualifying hand is Q-3-2, as shown below.

When the dealer has a qualifying hand, the game proceeds in a normal manner. That is, you have to beat the dealer's hand to win both the ante and play bets (at even money). If your hand is a straight or better, you are also paid the ante bonus. If the dealer's hand beats yours, you lose both the ante and the play wagers but, if your hand is good enough, you still win the ante bonus. All ties are pushes in which no money changes hands.

Whenever the dealer's hand is not qualified, the dealer folds and pays even money on just the ante bet. The play bet is returned to you and the ante bonus still pays off. In either case, if you made a Pair Plus bet you will be paid according to the Pair Plus bonus paytable.

TABLE ETIQUETTE

Three Card Poker is a fast-moving game. To avoid annoying the other players, you should stay alert and try not to hold up the action. Because of the game's simplicity and its uncomplicated strategy, this should not be hard to do.

When you sit down and have obtained some chips from the dealer, the first thing you have to do is place a wager. The bet may be put either on the ante spot or the Pair Plus circle, or a bet on each. Place your bets as soon as the dealer has collected all the cards from the previous round. Unless you feel very lucky, follow our strategy advice and bet the table minimum.

After all the cards have been dealt, look at your three cards. Since it is against casino rules to show your cards to anyone else, make a reasonable attempt to shield them. Make your bet-or-fold decision quickly enough so as not to hold up the game. This is easy to do if you apply our simple strategy rules.

If you decide to fold, toss your cards (face down) toward the dealer. She will place them in the discard stack and remove your ante. If you decide to bet, place the same amount as your ante on the PLAY box and lay your cards face-down next to the bet. Now you are done, and the dealer takes over. The dealer will turn over each active player's cards, in turn, and make the appropriate payoffs. Dealers do make mistakes; so keep alert to be sure you are getting the proper bonuses.

Tipping, of course, is a matter of personal preference. Instead of tipping a dealer directly, you may prefer to place a bet for the dealer. In Three Card Poker, however, because of the two-tier betting procedure, placing a bet for the dealer is discouraged. If you want to tip the dealer, it is simpler to just toss her a chip.

4 – THE PAYOFFS

THE ANTE BONUS
The ante bonus is paid even if the dealer beats your hand. The ante bonus is also paid if the dealer does not qualify, which is an improvement over Caribbean Stud. If your hand is a straight or better, you are paid a bonus on your ante wager in accordance with the following schedule:

ANTE BONUS PAYTABLE	
HAND	**PAYS**
Straight Flush	5 to 1
Three of a Kind	4 to 1
Straight	1 to 1

Let's say your ante and play bets are $10 each and you are dealt three-of-a-kind, but the dealer beats you with a straight flush. Because the dealer has a better hand, you lose the ante and play bets; however, you still win a 4 to 1 bonus on the ante bet, which amounts to $40. Your net gain for this hand is $40 - $10(ante) - $10(play) = $20. Somehow, I am attracted to a game that pays off even when I have a losing hand!

THE PAIR PLUS BONUS

The Pair Plus is a side bet that pays according to the value of your hand and is independent of the game itself. An unusual aspect of Three Card Poker is that the Pair Plus side bet can be played *instead* of the main game. That is, if a Pair Plus bet is placed, the ante bet becomes optional. If you placed a Pair Plus bet and are dealt a pair or better, you will be paid according to the following schedule:

PAIR PLUS BONUS PAYTABLE	
HAND	**PAYS**
Straight Flush	40 to 1
Three of a Kind	30 to 1
Straight	6 to 1
Flush	4 to 1
Pair	1 to 1

Anything less than a pair and you lose the Pair Plus wager (that's why its called *Pair Plus*). On average, you can expect to get a paying Pair Plus hand about once in every four deals. If you don't ante and only place a bet in the Pair Plus circle, you are essentially cutting the dealer out of the equation. The dealer's hand becomes immaterial because you are strictly playing against the Pair Plus bonus paytable.

5 — WINNING HANDS

The poker rankings in Three Card Poker are similar to standard poker except that a triplet beats a straight, and a straight beats a flush. Since the hand contains only three cards, many standard poker hands such as two-pairs, a full house, or four-of-a-kind can not exist. Three Card Poker uses one standard 52-card deck with no wild cards. The value of a hand depends on which of the following card combinations it contains, listed in order from the highest to the lowest:

Straight Flush:

Three consecutive cards, all of the same suit, as shown below. A-K-Q is the highest straight flush and A-2-3 is the lowest. The odds of being dealt a three-card straight flush are 1 in 460 hands.

Should the dealer and a player both have straight flushes, the hand containing the highest-ranking card is the winner. If both the dealer and player have identical straight flushes (except for the suit), it is a push.

Three-of-a-Kind:

Three cards of the same rank, as shown below. The odds of being dealt three of a kind are about 1 in 425 hands.

Should the dealer and a player both have three of a kind, the one with the highest rank is the winner.

Straight:
Three consecutive cards of mixed suits, as shown below. An ace may be either the lowest card as in A-2-3 or the highest card as in A-K-Q. The odds of being dealt a three-card straight are 1 in 31 hands. Keep in mind that three-of-a-kind beats a straight.

Should the dealer and a player both have straights, the one containing the highest ranked card is the winner. If the highest ranked card in both hands is the same, it is a push.

Flush:
Three cards of the same suit, not in sequence, as shown below. The odds of being dealt a three-card flush are 1 in 20 hands. Keep in mind that a flush is beat by three-of-a-kind or a straight.

Should the dealer and a player both have flushes, the one containing the highest ranked card is the winner. If the highest ranked card in both hands is the same, then the second- and third-highest ranked cards are the tiebreakers.

Pair: Two cards of the same rank. The remaining card is unrelated. The odds of being dealt a pair are about 1 in 6 hands. On average, you will be dealt a pair *or better* every fourth hand.

The highest-ranked pair wins. If two hands contain pairs of the same rank, then the one with the highest-ranked odd card wins. If all cards are the same rank, it is a push.

Queen-high:
A hand that contains none of the above poker hands, but does have one Queen, as shown below. The two remaining cards are unrelated. The odds of being dealt a Queen-high *or better* are about 1 in 2.3 hands. That means the dealer will qualify about 44% of the time.

Low Cards:
A hand that contains none of the above poker hands, but has mixed cards no higher than one Jack, as shown below. The odds of being dealt a Jack or lower hand are about 1 in 3.3 hands.

This is a non-qualifying hand for the dealer.

6 — PLAYING STRATEGY

Like most of the new games, Three Card Poker is a negative expectation game. There is no strategy that will overcome the house edge and make the game profitable for the player. Sure, sometimes a sloppy dealer will inadvertently expose her bottom card, but that does not happen very often. (More about that later.)

To make your bankroll last as long as possible (until you hit that winning streak), you need to apply good playing strategy. The Three Card Poker player has three basic decisions to make: (1) how much money to ante, (2) whether or not to place the Pair Plus bet, and (3) whether to continue playing after seeing the cards or fold the hand and lose the ante. Each of these three choices will affect how fast you lose your money.

A PERFECTLY SIMPLE STRATEGY

For each game in this book, we have tried to present a perfect or near-perfect strategy, as well as a simple strategy so that inexperienced players can get started quickly. Fortunately, the perfect strategy for Three Card Poker is so easy that we only need the one version, which we call *a perfectly simple strategy*.

It is summarized as follows:

A PERFECTLY SIMPLE STRATEGY
for Three Card Poker

Rule 1: Ante the table minimum.
Rule 2: Pair Plus bet is optional.
Rule 3: Call your hand if it contains a Queen or better. Otherwise, fold.

This is clearly the simplest strategy of any table game requiring player decisions. To show that these rules are valid, we will analyze each one.

Rule 1.

Since Three Card Poker is a negative expectation game, the more you bet, the faster you will lose. The lowest table minimum you are likely to find is $5. Try to play at those tables. The only time to raise your ante is when you clearly hit a winning streak.

Rule 2.

The Pair Plus wager is called optional because, although it is a negative expectation gamble, the house edge is only 2.3%. Since you don't get to make any playing decisions, there is no strategy and the outcome of the wager is purely dependent on luck.

Rule 3.

This is the basic call-fold playing strategy, and it couldn't be easier to remember. Yes, it does mimic the dealer's qualification rule, but in this case it works just fine. To be mathematically precise, the call-fold breakpoint should actually be **queen-6-4**. If you want to remember queen-6-4 instead of queen, that's okay, but the difference in the house edge is less than one-tenth of a%.

SEEING OTHER CARDS

As we have mentioned before, the rule is that you are not supposed to show your cards to any other players. Because of sloppy card handling, it is sometimes easy to get glimpses of other cards. However, this is usually not very helpful, and sometimes can lead you into making incorrect strategy decisions.

The general rule is that if you see at least three player's cards that are Queen or higher, the dealer is less apt to qualify. You can then risk calling a hand that you would normally fold.

On the other hand, if you see one of the *dealer's* cards, you can get a significant edge. When distributing the three-card stacks from the shuffling machine, an inattentive or inexperienced dealer may expose the bottom card. If you see the dealer's bottom card, you should do the following:

- Dealer's card is a jack or less: Call all hands.
- Dealer's card is a queen: Call with queen-9 or better.
- Dealer's card is a king: Call with king-9 or better.
- Dealer's card is an ace: Call with ace-9 or better.

This is a rare situation, but it can be profitable to be prepared. When it occurs, it can give you more than a 3% edge over the house.

CONCLUSION

Three card Poker is a fun and easy game to play. It pays nice bonuses for the better hands, which pay out even if the dealer does not qualify. It moves along quickly and smoothly and has no rules that are annoying or irritating to the players. Although the speed of play makes the game nice and lively, it also carries with it some danger. The 3.4% house edge on the basic game will grind down your bankroll faster than most table games. However, the game is a pleasant diversion and if you are lucky, you might hit a nice Pair Plus bonus.

V. PAI GOW POKER

1 — OVERVIEW

Pai Gow Poker is an American version of the old Chinese game of Pai Gow. Actually, it is a blending of Pai Gow and poker that, in its earliest form, probably dates back to the mid-1800s. In 1986, a modern version of Pai Gow Poker got it's start in California card rooms and, in 1987, the casino version (in which the house may act as banker) was introduced in Las Vegas. A few years later, the New Jersey Casino Control Commission approved Pai Gow Poker. Since then, it has become one of the fastest-growing games in American casinos.

The original game of Pai Gow, which uses special dominos, is symbolic, enigmatic, and difficult to learn. Pai Gow Poker, on the other hand, uses a regular deck of cards and is based on standard poker hands. It is comparatively easy to learn and play—our casinos wouldn't have it any other way.

Pai Gow Poker is played on a blackjack-like table with six player positions. It uses a standard 52-card deck plus one joker. With a couple of exceptions, winning hands are almost the same as standard poker hands. That is where the similarity to poker ends because you only play against the banker's hand, and you have only one opportunity to place a bet. Consequently, the bluffing and normal playing strategies that are used in regular poker games are of no value.

The game begins after the banker is selected and each player puts up an initial bet. The selection procedure for the banker, who may be the dealer or one of the players, will be explained later. Seven cards are then dealt to everyone at the table, including the dealer. You now have to split your seven cards into two separate hands: a two-card hand and a five-card hand. The poker value of the five-card hand must be higher than the two-card hand.

You win if both hands *beat* both of the banker's hands. If one hand beats the banker and the other doesn't, it is considered a push and no money changes hands. Hands that are exactly alike are called copy hands and are won by the banker. Although the house already has the edge (unless a player is the banker), to be certain it can never lose money, it assesses a 5% commission on all winning bets.

Pai Gow Poker moves at a pretty leisurely pace. Originally, the dealing process was somewhat involved and convoluted, and many players are very slow and deliberate in deciding how to split their hands. Today, however, most casinos have figured out ways to speed up the game and most players are experienced enough to arrange their hands quickly. Your bankroll will fluctuate less than in other games because all the bets are even money, and almost half the hands are pushes.

In the following sections, you will learn the rules of play, who gets to be the banker, the advantages of being a banker, how special situations are handled, and the best strategy for splitting your hand. You will also get information on special bonuses, which vary from casino to casino. Taking the time to read and learn about these things is the best chance you have of being a winner.

2 — FUNDAMENTALS OF PLAY

THE PLAYING TABLE
Pai Gow Poker is played on a table that is similar to a blackjack table and is usually located in or near the blackjack area. In many casinos it is easy to find because there is an elevated sign at the table identifying the game. There are six player positions around the curved side of the table (see Fig. 3). The dealer stands at the flat side with a chip rack directly in front of her and a shuffling machine to her right.

The older tables have a row of marked spaces where the dealt hands are first placed. To either side of the spaces are commission boxes marked 1,2,3 and 4,5,6. You won't, however, see such markings on the newer tables. To speed up the game, most casinos have dispensed with the intermediate dealing and commission collection steps. Originally three dice were rolled before each deal to determine which player received the first hand. (The player positions are marked 1 through 6.) Now most casinos use a random number generator that reveals a new number at the start of every deal. This number is usually displayed in a window on the surface of the table.

At each player position is a betting circle where your bet should be placed. Below the betting circle are two boxes where your two hands should be laid face down after splitting them. The lower box, which is marked HIGH, is where to place your five-card hand, and the upper box, marked 2nd HIGHEST, is where to place your two-card hand.

HOW THE GAME IS PLAYED
The object in Pai Gow Poker is to arrange your seven cards to make the best combination of five-card and two-card poker hands that you can. This is called *setting the hand*. The only rule is that your five-card hand *must* have a poker value higher than your

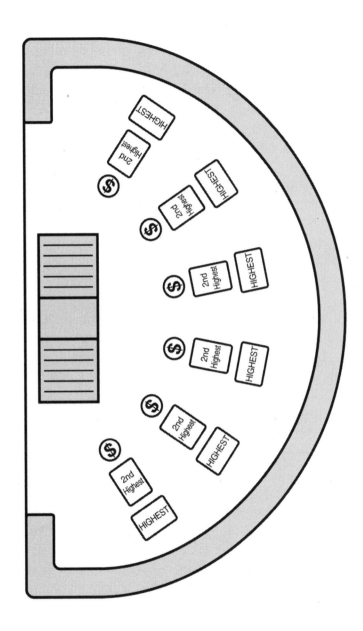

Figure 4 - Typical Pai Gow Table

two-card hand. If it does not, your bet is forfeited. Your bet is also forfeited if you do not lay out your two hands properly. The two-card hand must be positioned above the five-card hand (from the player's viewpoint). After all the players have set their hands, the dealer turns over her cards and sets her hand according to specific house rules.

All players bet against the bank, therefore, the goal of the game is for both of your hands to beat both of the banker's hands. To win, your two-card hand must have a higher poker value than the banker's two-card hand, and your five-card hand must have a higher value than the banker's five-card hand. Should one of your hands exactly match the banker's hand, it is called a *copy*, and the banker wins all copies. If you win one hand, but lose the other, it is considered a push and no money changes hands.

To illustrate the effect of a copy, suppose you beat the banker's five-card hand and you both have a two-card ace-queen. This is a push because the two-card hand, being a copy, is won by the banker. On the other hand, if the banker's five-card hand was better than yours, you lost because both of your hands were beat.

The game begins after all the players have placed their wagers. The minimum bet requirement in most casinos can range any-where from $10 to $100, although you may find a $5 minimum in some smaller places. The dealer then shuffles the cards (usu-ally with the aid of a shuffling machine) and deals out seven hands of seven cards each. All hands are dealt regardless of the number of players at the table. The first hand is given to the player designated by the number-generator display, and the re-maining hands are dealt counter-clockwise from that position. (Some casinos deal in a clockwise direction.) Finally, the cards at vacant player positions are removed by the dealer.

The bank is offered to each player, in turn, and that player may accept or pass. If a player declines the bank, the dealer will always take the player's turn and act as banker for that hand. The dealer is included in the rotation of the bank, so that it is offered to each player on every seventh hand. A white plastic marker identifies the current banker.

After the cards are dealt and the banker selection formalities are concluded, it is time to examine your hand. You should arrange (set) your cards into a two-card (2nd highest) hand and a five-card (high) hand as described above. The dealer does not look at her cards until everyone else has set their hands and placed them face down in the designated spaces. The dealer then turns over her seven cards and sets her hand.

The dealer's hand is the first one to be compared against the banker's (unless the dealer is the banker). Then the remaining hands are compared against the banker's hand, and the bets are settled by the dealer. The dealer makes all the payouts and collections, whether or not the dealer is the banker. Winning hands are paid even money, less a five-percent commission. Losing hands lose the amount wagered. A commission is not charged against losing or tie hands.

Although the dealer represents the casino and handles the cards and the payoffs, from the standpoint of playing the game she is just another player at the table. Her hand is on an equal footing with the other players hands. The casino earns its profit from the five-percent commission. The hand you have to beat is the banker's, who may or may not be the dealer.

Finally, don't be put off by the ritualistic procedures and seeming complexity of the game. This stuff is all handled by the dealer. All you have to do is put up your wager and set your hand. In most ways it is simpler to play than blackjack.

THE BANKER

Each time a hand is dealt, the position of the bank rotates one step counter-clockwise (clockwise in some casinos). As we mentioned earlier, the dealer is included in the rotation, so each player gets the opportunity to be banker on every seventh hand. The dealer substitutes as banker for any player that passes and for all vacant player positions. A white plastic marker indicates the current position of the bank.

A few casinos have different procedures for determining how often a player gets to be banker. When no other players want the bank, some casinos will allow you to bank as often as every other hand. If you accept the bank, you must be able and willing to cover all wagers on the table. If you cannot cover all the bets, most casinos will agree to co-bank with you on a 50-50 basis. When co-banking, the banker's cards have to be set according to the casino rules.

When you accept the bank, you are betting against all the other players *and* the house. The dealer will place a bet for the house equal to your previous bet. You may request to have this bet reduced to the table minimum. In some casinos, you may decline to bet against the house. There is no good reason for doing this, however, since you have the same advantage (you win all copies) over the house that you have over the other players.

Whenever you assume the bank, the dealer continues to handle all the chips and makes the necessary payouts and collections. At the end of each hand, you are charged a 5% commission against your net aggregate winnings; that is, the total wins minus the losses.

Getting a poor hand while acting as banker could be very costly. So why would anyone assume such a risk? Because, in the long run, being banker gives you an edge over the other players—

just like the casino's edge. That is, you win all copy hands. For this reason, professionals and expert players try to bank as often as possible.

SETTING THE HAND

Although the basic method for setting a Pai Gow Poker hand has already been explained, this section will cover more detail to give you a deeper understanding of the procedure. Pai Gow Poker uses a standard 52-card deck plus one joker. The joker may only be used as an ace or to complete a straight, a flush, or a straight flush. When used in a straight or straight flush, the joker becomes the rank and suit of the card needed to complete the hand. When used in a flush, it becomes the highest ranking missing card of the flush suit. It can never be used as part of a pair, three-of-a-kind, four-of-a-kind, or five-of-a-kind for any card other than an ace. If it is used alone, the joker becomes an ace. In poker parlance, such a joker is known as a *bug*.

To reiterate, you are dealt seven cards, which you arrange to make two hands: a two-card hand and a five-card hand. The poker value of the five-card hand must be higher than the two-card hand. Since this can be done in more than one way, the object is to set the two hands so that they have the best chance of beating the banker's two hands. The highest possible five-card hand is five aces, which consists of the four aces and the joker. The highest two-card hand is a pair of aces. The two-card hand cannot be a straight or a flush.

When you first receive your cards, the best procedure is to arrange them in order, from the highest rank to the lowest rank. Then look for the possibility of a flush or a straight. If you were dealt the joker, check to see if it can complete a flush or straight, or make a pair of aces. Finally, look for pairs and triplets. Once you have reviewed the hand and are aware of all the possible combinations, set it according to the strategy rules shown later.

When you have decided how to set your hand, place the cards face down in two stacks with the two-card hand above the five-card hand. At every player position there are two boxes. The one marked HIGH is where the five-card hand goes, and the one marked 2nd HIGHEST is where the two-card hand goes. The five-card hand is sometimes referred to as the back hand, and the two-card hand is sometimes called the low hand or the front hand.

You should be very careful and deliberate when setting your hand. This is especially true when it contains the joker. The basic idea is to make the two-card hand as high as possible without exceeding the value of the five-card hand. If you don't have good enough cards to make two winning hands, you should try for a push by forming one hand that will not lose. For example, if you are dealt the following cards:

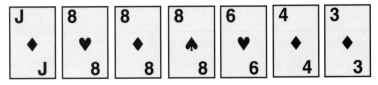

It is pretty obvious that you should five-card the three eight's and two-card the highest odd cards, as follows:

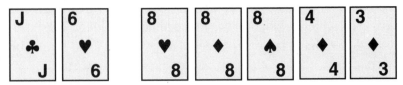

Although the J-6 is a losing hand, you don't have any other option. Since the five-card hand has an 85% chance of winning, you will at least push.

If you are dealt two pairs (and nothing else worthwhile) you should sometimes split the pairs, depending on the ranks of the odd cards.

In the following hand...

you should split the pairs by putting the fives in the two-card hand.

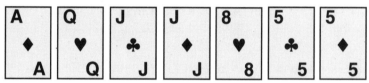

This is necessary because keeping the pairs together in the five-card hand would result in an unacceptably weak two-card hand of 8-3, which is an almost certain loser. On the other hand, if the odd cards are strong enough as in the following hand...

the two pairs should be kept together, as follows:

The A-Q is a reasonably strong two-card hand and the J-J-5-5 is a very strong five-card hand with an 81% of winning.

The following is an example of how easy it is to misplay a hand that contains a joker:

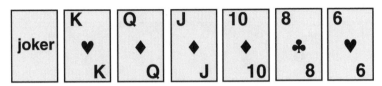

In this hand, don't make the mistake of misplaying the joker by five-carding an ace-high straight. As you will see in the section on strategy, you should make the two-card hand as high as possible without compromising the five-card hand. Thus, the best way to set this hand is as follows:

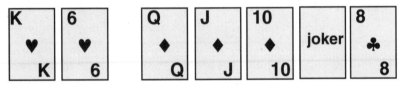

Although it will probably lose, a K-6 is still a lot better than 8-6. Whether the straight is ace-high or queen-high doesn't really matter because either one has a better than 90% chance of winning.

These are only a few examples to give you a taste of how the cards should be set. Later, you will be shown the best setting rules for players. You will also be shown the house rules that the dealers use to set their cards.

DEALER ASSISTANCE

If you can't figure out the best way to set your cards, you may ask the dealer for assistance. The dealer will suggest how to set them according to the house rules, but will not take responsibility for winning or losing hands. If one of the other players is the banker, you should avoid doing this because seeing your cards will give that person a distinct advantage in setting his own hand (he knows what he has to beat), especially if there are few players at the table.

PLAYING TWO HANDS

In some table games you are permitted to play multiple hands. In Pai Gow Poker, however, most casinos allow you to play only one hand at a time. A few casinos circulate a *Dragon* marker when there are one or more vacant player positions. When you are offered the Dragon marker, you may play a second hand if you wish. If you accept, you may wager any amount on the second hand so long as it is at least half of your original bet.

You must set your original hand first, and then set the second hand. Any benefit comes from the fact that you get to see a total of 14 cards (over 26% of the deck), which may be an advantage for setting the second hand. Since the opportunity for playing a second hand is small, we are only making you aware that it exists and are not providing any specific strategy information.

ADDITIONAL BETTORS

In Pai Gow Poker, it is permissible for another person to place a side bet on your hand, if you agree. This person may be a bystander or another player at your table. Whenever you give such permission (and it is customary to do so), you still maintain full control on how your hand is set. In some casinos, the floor supervisor must also give permission. When extra betting occurs, the total amount wagered on your betting circle cannot exceed the table limit.

TABLE ETIQUETTE

Before sitting down at any new table game for the first time, it is always a good idea to stand nearby and watch several rounds of play. This is especially true for Pai Gow Poker. When you do sit down, just watch what the other players are doing and try to do the same. If you make a mistake in table protocol, the dealer will politely correct you.

The first thing you should do (after you get chips from the dealer) is to place your bet. Put the bet directly on the bet circle any time after the dealer has collected all the cards from the previous round. If the bank is offered to you, decline it unless you are a very experienced player.

After all the cards have been dealt, look at your seven cards. It is against casino rules to show your cards to anyone else, and it is also against your best interest to do so. Set your cards carefully, but try not to hold up the game. You usually have plenty of time because some players are unhurried and may even ask the dealer for help.

When you set your cards be sure that the five-card hand is the better hand and that you place it below the two-card hand. If you fail to do these things correctly, you will automatically lose your bet. You will also lose your bet if you miscount the cards when you split the hand, such as 3-4 instead of 2-5. The player is penalized for making mistakes; the dealer and the banker are not.

Once the banker's or the dealer's cards are exposed, you cannot touch yours. From this point on, the dealer handles all the cards.

3 – WINNING HANDS

The various card combinations that produce winning hands in Pai Gow Poker are similar to regular poker. The main exception involves straights and straight flushes (see below). Pai Gow Poker uses one standard 52-card deck with one joker. The joker can only be used as an ace, or to complete a flush, straight, straight flush, or royal flush. Suits have no relative value; they only come into play for a flush, a straight flush, or a royal flush.

FIVE-CARD HAND

The value of a five-card hand depends on which of the following card combinations it contains, listed in order from the highest to the lowest:

Five Aces:
Four aces and the joker, as shown below, is the highest value hand in Pai Gow Poker. Since there is only one way to make this hand, it is very rare.

Royal Flush:
An ace-high straight flush, as shown below, is the second-highest hand in Pai Gow Poker. The joker may be used to complete a royal flush.

Since suits do not have any relative value, two royal flushes of different suits constitute a copy. Copies are won by the banker.

Straight Flush:
Five consecutive cards, all of the same suit, as shown below. The joker may be used to complete a straight flush.

Should the banker and a player both have straight flushes, the higher-valued one is the winner. In Pai Gow Poker, an A-2-3-4-5 is the best straight flush and a king-high is the second best straight flush. The hand shown above is a jack-high straight flush. If both the banker and player have identical straight flushes (except for the suit), then the banker wins.

NOTE: Some casinos use standard poker rankings so that the best straight flush is king-high, and the lowest is A-2-3-4-5.

Four-of-a-Kind:
Four cards of the same rank, as shown below. The fifth card is unrelated to the others. Except for aces, the joker cannot be used to convert three-of-a-kind to four-of-a-kind.

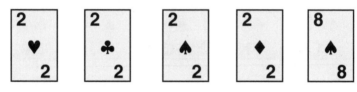

Should the banker and a player both have four of a kind, the hand with the highest rank is the winner.

Full House:
Three cards of the same rank and two cards of another rank, that is, three-of-a-kind and a pair. Except for aces, the joker cannot be used to complete a full house.

Should the banker and a player both have a full house, the hand with the highest ranked three of a kind is the winner. The ranks of the pairs are immaterial.

Flush:

Five cards of the same suit, not in sequence, as shown below. The joker may be used to complete a flush. For the purpose of breaking a tie, the joker is considered to be an ace.

Should the banker and a player both have flushes, the one containing the highest ranked card is the winner. If the highest ranked card in both hands is the same, then the second-highest ranked card is the tiebreaker. If that is also the same, then the third-, the fourth-, and the fifth-highest cards are compared. If all five cards in both hands are the same rank, that is considered a copy and the banker wins.

Straight:

Five consecutive cards of mixed suits, as shown below. The joker may be used to complete a straight.

Should the banker and a player both have straights, the higher-valued one is the winner. In Pai Gow Poker, an A-K-Q-J-10 is the best straight, an A-2-3-4-5 is the second-best straight, and a king-high is the third-best straight. If both hands have identical straights, the banker wins.

NOTE: Some casinos use standard poker rankings so that the second-best straight is king-high, and the lowest is A-2-3-4-5.

Three-of-a-Kind:

Three cards of the same rank, as shown below. The remaining two cards are unrelated. Except for aces, the joker cannot be used to convert a pair to three-of-a-kind.

Should the banker and a player both have three of a kind, the one with the highest rank is the winner.

Two Pairs:

A pair of one rank and a pair of another rank, as shown below. The fifth card is unrelated. Again, except for aces, the joker cannot be used to make a pair.

Should both the banker and a player have two pairs, the one with the highest-ranked pair is the winner. If the highest-ranked pairs are the same, then the one having the highest-ranked second pair wins. If both pairs are the same rank, then the hand with the highest fifth card wins. If all cards are the same rank, the banker wins.

One Pair:

Two cards of the same rank, as shown below. The three remaining cards are unrelated.

The highest-ranked pair wins. If the banker's and player's five-card hands contain pairs of the same rank, then the one with the highest-ranked odd card wins. If that card is the same, then the fourth and fifth cards break the tie in the hands. If all cards are the same rank, the banker wins.

High Card:
A hand that contains none of the above poker hands. The highest-ranked card in the hand determines its relative value.

If the banker and a player have the same high card, then the second, third, fourth, and fifth cards break the tie. Of course, if all cards are the same rank, the banker wins.

TWO-CARD HAND
As you would guess, flushes, straights, and straight flushes are not valid in two-card hands. Multiples of a particular rank above one pair are not possible. The value of a two-card hand depends on which of the following card combinations it contains, listed in order from the highest to the lowest:

One Pair:
Two cards of the same rank, as shown below. The best two-card hand is a pair of aces.

If the banker's and player's hands contain pairs of the same rank, the banker wins.

High Card:
A two-card hand that does not contain a pair. The highest-ranked card in the hand determines its relative value.

If the banker and a player have the same high card, then the second card breaks the tie. If both cards are the same rank, the banker wins.

4 – PLAYING STRATEGY

The primary strategy in playing Pai Gow Poker is how to set your hand. A mathematically-perfect strategy is far too complicated for anyone to memorize. In fact, such a strategy has never been published. One reason for this is that its exactness depends on the particular house setting rules that are used, and these vary somewhat from casino to casino.

The two strategies outlined in this section are a *simple strategy* and a *long strategy*. In addition, for reference purposes, an example of typical house rules for setting the dealer's hand is shown at the end of the section.

To simplify the wording of the strategy rules, the verbs *two-card* and *five-card* are extensively used. For example, in a hand containing two pairs, "two-card the smaller pair" means to put the smaller of the two pairs into the two-card hand. It is assumed that the remaining five cards are put into the five-card hand.

A *singleton* is an odd card that is not a part of a poker combination such as a pair, a triplet, a straight, or a flush. For instance, a hand containing two pairs and no other combinations, will have three singletons.

A SIMPLE STRATEGY

At first, you may wonder what is so simple about the following strategy. After you see the long strategy, you may think it is *too* simple. The simple strategy only covers the most common hands. This works because 85% of the hands dealt contain no pair, one pair, two pairs, or a triplet. The more infrequent hands such as three pairs or two triplets are so strong that you will likely win even if you don't set them exactly right.

SIMPLE PLAYING STRATEGY
for Pai Gow Poker

General Rule 1: Set the 2-card hand as high as possible without compromising the 5-card hand.

General Rule 2: Break-even for 2 cards is **A-8**. Break-even for 5 cards is **J-J**. Try to exceed break-even on both hands.

Specific common hands:

High card — Two-card the 2nd- and 3rd-highest cards.

One pair — Two-card the 2 highest singletons.

Two pairs — Without singleton Ace: Always split pairs. — With singleton Ace: Split J-J, 7-7 or better.

Three-of-a-kind — Split A-A-A. Do not split other triplets.

Straight— Five-card the lowest 5 cards in straight.

Flush — Five-card the lowest 5 cards in flush. Split flush, as necessary, to meet Rule 2.

These strategy rules are greatly simplified, but General Rules 1 and 2 will carry you a long way, especially if you have read the other material and developed a general understanding on how best to set hands. To be sure that you understand the above rules, we will analyze each one.

GENERAL RULE 1.

Set the 2-card hand as high as possible without compromising the 5-card hand. This rule will set your hand correctly 60% of the time. Just remember that that the five-card hand *must* be a higher poker value than the two-card hand. Also, remember that the joker is the same as an ace, unless it is completing a flush, straight, or straight flush.

GENERAL RULE 2.

Break-even for 2 cards is **A-8**. *Break-even for 5 cards is* **J-J**. *Try to exceed break-even on both hands.* It is important to remember these break-even hands. Break-even means that you have a 50% chance of winning the hand. If both hands are above break-even, you have a good chance of winning money. Knowing the break-even points will keep you out of trouble, especially for the more complex hands.

High card. *Two-card the 2nd- and 3rd-highest cards.* For instance, if you have K-J-10-7-5-4-3, two-card the J-10 and five-card the K-7-5-4-3.

One pair. *Two-card the two highest singletons.* This means that the pair goes in the five-card hand along with the three lowest singletons. For instance, if you have K-J-J-9-7-5-4, two-card the K-9 and five-card the J-J-7-5-4.

Two pairs. A two-pair hand is the one involving the most complex strategy. A glance at the long strategy in the next section makes this very apparent. We managed to boil the two-pairs strategy down to two simple rules. Although, this is the area of greatest simplification, these two rules should serve the casual and recreational player well.

> *Without singleton Ace: Always split pairs.* For instance, if you have Q-Q-J-9-4-4-2, two-card the 4-4 and five-card the Q-Q-J-9-2.

With singleton Ace: Split J-J, 7-7 or better. For instance, if you have A-Q-Q-J-9-9-4, two-card the 9-9 and five-card the A-Q-Q-J-4. If you have A-Q-Q-J-9-4-4, two-card the A-J and five-card the Q-Q-9-4-4.

Three of a kind. *Split A-A-A. Do not split other triplets.* For instance, if you have joker-A-A-Q-9-8-4, two-card the joker-Q or A-Q (it makes no difference) and five-card a pair of aces. If you have K-J-J-J-9-8-4, two-card the K-9 and five-card the J-J-J-8-4.

Straight. *Five-card the lowest 5 cards in straight.* For instance, if you have K-Q-J-10-9-8-5, two-card the K-5 and five-card the Q-J-10-9-8.

Flush. *Five-card the lowest 5 cards in flush. Split, as necessary, to meet Rule 2.* For instance, if you have joker A♥ Q♦ 10♠ 9♠ 7♠ 5♠, two-card the A♥ Q♦ and five-card the joker 10♠ 9♠ 7♠ 5♠. Although you broke up the pair of aces, both hands are above break-even. If you have A♠ Q♦ Q♠ J♥ 7♠ 5♠ 4♠, split the flush and two-card the A♠ J♥. Both hands are above break-even. If, instead, we saved the flush, the resulting Q♦ J♥ hand would be below break-even.

THE LONG STRATEGY

The following rules do not represent perfect playing strategy, which is far too complicated for the average player to memorize, but represent an accurate approximation. These are the rules you really need to know if you want to become a serious Pai Gow Poker player.

High card — A hand consisting of seven unrelated cards (singletons), with no flush, no straight, and no pairs.
    Two-card the second- and third-highest cards.
    If the two highest cards are A-K or A-Q, two-card the second- and fourth-highest cards

One pair — Five singletons with no flush and no straight. This is the most common hand in Pai Gow Poker.

Two-card the two highest singletons.

Two pairs — Three singletons with no flush and no straight. To split means: two-card the smaller pair and five-card the remaining cards.

High pair is A-A: Split.

High pair is K-K: Split.

Except if low pair is 5-5 thru 2-2 with A-J or higher: Two-card the highest singletons.

High pair is Q-Q: Split.

Except if low pair is 9-9 thru 2-2 with A-J or higher: Two-card the highest singletons.

High pair is J-J: Split.

Except with A-J or higher: Two-card the highest singletons.

High pair is 9-9 or 10-10: Split.

Except with singleton ace: Two-card the highest singletons.

High pair is 6-6 to 8-8: Split.

Except with singleton king or better: Two-card the highest singletons.

High pair is 3-3 to 5-5: Split.

Except with singleton queen or better: Two-card the highest singletons.

Three pairs — Plus one singleton.

Two-card the highest pair.

Three of a kind — Four singletons with no flush and no straight. To split means: break the triplet and five-card the resulting pair.

A-A-A: Split and two-card one ace plus the highest singleton.

K-K-K with J-10 or higher: Two-card the highest singletons.

K-K-K with J-9 or lower: Split and two-card one king plus the highest singleton.

Q-Q-Q: Two-card the highest singletons.

Straight — Two singletons with no flush and no pair. May include the joker.

Five-card the straight

For a six- or seven-card straight, five-card the lowest-value straight.

Flush — Two singletons with no straight and no pair. May include the joker.

Five-card the flush

For a six- or seven-card flush, five-card the lowest-value flush.

Straight or flush, with external pair — The pair is external to the straight or flush.

Two-card the pair, five-card the straight or flush.

Straight and included pair, no joker — One of the pair is shared by the straight.

Six- or seven-card straight: Five-card the lowest five cards of the straight.

Hand contains no Ace: Five-card the straight.

Ace-high straight with Q-Q, J-J, or 10-10: Five-card the pair and two-card the A-K.

Ace-high straight with A-A or K-K: Five-card the straight.

Straight and included pair, with joker — One of the pair is shared by the straight.

Ace or joker not needed to complete straight: Five-card the straight.

Ace-joker pair needed to complete ace-high straight: Five-card the ace and joker plus three lowest singletons.

Ace-joker pair needed to complete ace-low straight: Five-card the straight.

Jack-high (or higher) joker straight: Five-card the pair.

Ten-high (or lower) joker straight: Five-card the straight.

Flush and included pair — One or two of the pair are shared by the flush.

Six- or seven-card flush: Five-card the lowest five cards of the flush.

Ace and/or joker not needed to complete flush: Five-card the flush.

Ace and/or joker needed to complete flush: Five-card the pair if second-highest card is 10 or better and pair is 10-10 or better. Otherwise, five-card the flush.

Straight and flush or straight flush — No pairs.

Five-card the straight or the flush, whichever leaves the highest two-card hand.

The rule is the same for a straight flush or royal.

Straight and flush and one pair — Or straight flush.

If possible, two-card the pair and five-card the straight or flush or straight flush.

If pair is included, use above rules for straight or flush with included pair.

Straight or flush and two pairs — Or straight flush.

If possible, two-card one of the pairs and five-card the straight or flush.

If both pairs are included, split the straight or flush and use above rules for two pairs.

Full house — Plus two singletons. May include the joker.

Split the full house and two-card the pair.

Three of a kind plus three of a kind — Plus one singleton.
Two-card a pair from the higher triplet and five-card the lower triplet.

Four of a kind — Plus three singletons.
A-A-A-A or K-K-K-K: Split the quad and two-card a pair.
Q-Q-Q-Q or J-J-J-J: With a singleton ace, five-card the quad. Otherwise split.
10-10-10-10 or 9-9-9-9: With a king or higher, five-card the quad. Otherwise split.
8-8-8-8 or 7-7-7-7: With queen or higher, five-card the quad. Otherwise split.
6-6-6-6 or lower: Five-card the quad.

Four of a kind plus one pair — Plus one singleton.
Five-card the quad and two-card the pair.
Exception: If quad is Q-Q-Q-Q or higher *and* pair is 4-4 or lower, two-card two of the quad and five-card two pairs.

Four of a kind plus three of a kind — No singletons.
Two-card the highest pair and five-card either a quad or a full house.

Five aces — Plus two singletons.
Two-card a pair of aces.

SEEING OTHER CARDS

The casino rule is that you are not supposed to show your cards to any other players. Is there any advantage to seeing other player's cards? Only for the banker, especially if the banker is another player. Theoretically, there is no advantage to the dealer because she has to set her hand strictly according to unvarying house rules. However, there is no assurance to the player that this always happens.

It would, without a doubt, be a tremendous advantage for a player to see the banker's cards. But, this is unlikely to ever happen.

Of course, the rule is broken whenever a player asks the dealer for help in setting his hand. This gives the banker/player a look at what he has to beat. It doesn't matter as much at a full table, because if the banker/player breaks strategy rules to beat the exposed hand, he might end up losing against more of the other hands. With only two or three players, however, there is a clear advantage.

OVERCOMING THE HOUSE EDGE

Aside from blackjack and, possibly, Spanish 21, Pai Gow Poker is the only other casino game in which it is theoretically possible to overcome the house edge. We used the modifier *theoretical* because from a practical standpoint, beating the house is not easy to do. However, because it *is* possible, this is a subject that needs to be addressed.

The theoretical possibility of beating the house is due to the fact that a banker/player in Pai Gow Poker can have as much as a 0.4% edge over the house under optimum conditions. Most of the time the advantage probably comes closer to 0.2%, but it is still an advantage. Besides winning all copy hands, the other benefit is that the 5% rake is applied to the net aggregate win (wins minus losses) instead of each individual win.

Since a player usually gets the opportunity to bank on every seventh hand, how is it possible to overcome the player's negative expectation of 2.5 to 2.8%? It ain't easy!

Obviously, the only way to overcome the house edge in Pai Gow Poker is by trying to bank as often as possible. And that alone is not enough.

The following conditions are necessary to have any chance of overcoming the house edge:

Necessary Conditions for a House Edge

A table in which the other players are betting heavily—considerably above the table minimum.

A table in which the players are all declining the bank and the dealer is willing to let you bank every second or third hand. This situation is no longer easy to find.

When not banking, you should wager no more than the table minimum.

When the above conditions are optimal, the long-term expectation can actually become positive. To succeed, however, you must fully understand the best playing strategy and your bankroll must be large enough to sustain potential losses when banking the game.

HOUSE RULES FOR SETTING CARDS

In casino parlance, the house setting rules are called the *house way*. The house way falls somewhere between the Simpler Strategy and the Long Strategy in complexity, and it is perfectly reasonable for you to apply the house rules for setting your own cards. The house way varies somewhat from casino to casino, but the rules shown below are typical.

NO PAIR —
Two-card the second- and third-highest cards.

ONE PAIR —
Two-card the two highest singletons.

TWO PAIRS —

When splitting, always two-card the lowest pair.

If high pair is A-A: Split.

Without singleton Ace:

Split if low pair is 7-7 or better.

With singleton Ace:

Split if high pair is J-J or better and low pair is 6-6 or better.

THREE PAIRS —

Two-card the highest pair.

THREE OF A KIND —

A-A-A: Split and two-card one ace plus the highest singleton.

Other triplets: Two-card the highest singletons.

THREE OF A KIND PLUS THREE OF A KIND —

Two-card a pair from the highest triplet.

STRAIGHTS, FLUSHES, AND STRAIGHT FLUSHES —

With a choice to play either a flush, straight, or straight flush, five-card the category that will allow two-carding the highest two cards.

With one pair: Two-card the pair if a straight, flush, or straight flush can be preserved.

With two pairs: If pairs are 10-10 or better, use two pairs rule. Otherwise, preserve the straight, flush, or straight flush.

With three pairs: Use three pairs rule.

With three-of-a-kind: Two-card a pair of the triplet.

With full house: Use full house rule.

FULL HOUSE —

Two-card the pair.

THREE-OF-A-KIND AND TWO PAIRS —
Two-card the highest pair.

FOUR-OF-A-KIND —
Jacks or better: Split and two-card a pair of the quad.
7's thru 10's: Two-card A-K, A-Q, A-J, or extra pair. Otherwise split.
2's thru 6's: Never split. Two-card highest singletons.

FIVE ACES —
Split and two-card a pair of aces. If hand contains a pair of kings, then two-card the kings.

CONCLUSION
Having gotten its start in the cardrooms of California, Pai Gow Poker is really a gambler's game. Nevada upped the rake to 5% so it is more difficult to beat the edge, even for a player who banks a lot. Yet, if you never take the bank, the house edge is only 2.8%, assuming you play correctly. Because all the betting is at even money and there are so many pushes, your bankroll will not fluctuate excessively. All in all, the game is a fun and leisurely experience that will not drain your bankroll at an excessive rate. Although the strategy can get somewhat complicated, Pai Gow Poker is basically a very simple game to play.

VI. SPANISH 21

1 — OVERVIEW

A child of the computer age, Spanish 21 is a computer-derived variation of blackjack. The term "Spanish" refers to the 48-card deck used in some Spanish card games. It is a regular 52-card deck with the four tens removed. Although, in most respects, Spanish 21 is played just like standard blackjack, the basic strategy is somewhat different.

As a specially-designed version of blackjack, Spanish 21 has liberalized rules and unique bonuses. The casinos can be so generous because removal of the four tens from the deck gives the house a large advantage. The changes in rules and payouts were designed to attract jaded blackjack players and are what has made the game so popular. For instance, in standard blackjack, it is always exhilarating to hit a count of 21 on the nose, but it quickly turns into a disappointment if the dealer also hits 21 (resulting in a push instead of a win). In Spanish 21, if both dealer and player have 21, the player wins! How exciting!

In addition, bonuses are paid for getting 21 with five cards, six cards, and seven cards, and for getting certain three-card combinations such as 6-7-8 and 7-7-7. Then there is the super bonus: If you get a suited 7-7-7 and the dealer's upcard is a 7, a bonus is paid to *all* the players at the table. It's no wonder that many blackjack players are migrating to Spanish 21.

Spanish 21 is played on a regular blackjack table. Except for the liberal payoffs, the game appears to be almost identical to standard blackjack. This is what fools some experienced blackjack players. The hidden differences are that the house edge is bigger and, most importantly, the basic strategy for standard blackjack does not work very well. To keep from losing your shirt, you have to learn a modified strategy.

Like regular blackjack, the game is easy to learn. You are dealt two cards and then take additional cards (hits) one-by-one, trying to get as close to a total count of 21 without going over. When all the players are through taking hits, the dealer does the same by a fixed set of rules. If you beat the dealer, you win even money. If you have the same card count as the dealer (except for a count of 21) it is a tie (called a push), and no money changes hands.

In the following sections, you will learn the rules of play, how special situations are handled, the probabilities of being dealt winning hands, and the best playing strategy. You will also get complete information on the bonuses and the super bonuses. Even if you are an experienced blackjack player, taking the time to read and learn about these things will improve your chances of being a winner.

2 — FUNDAMENTALS OF PLAY

THE PLAYING TABLE
Spanish 21 is played on a table that is essentially identical to a standard blackjack table and is located in the blackjack area. In most casinos it is easy to find because there is an elevated sign at the table identifying the game. The table has six or seven player positions around the curved side of the table (see Fig. 4). The dealer stands at the flat side with a chip rack directly in front of

her and a card-dealing shoe to her left.

At each player position is one betting spot in the shape of a circle or a rectangle. This is where your initial bet should be placed. You can make additional bets by splitting pairs or doubling down, and such additional bets are placed alongside the original bet.

HOW THE GAME IS PLAYED

As in standard blackjack, the goal in Spanish 21 is to build a hand in which your cards add up to a total value higher than the dealer's hand, without exceeding a count of 21. While you are doing this, there are other actions that can be taken, such as doubling your bet, splitting pairs, or surrendering your hand.

The Deck

The 48-card deck used in Spanish 21 is standard except that all four tens have been removed. Removing the tens effectively reduces the number of ten-value cards by 25%, giving the dealer a major mathematical advantage. Six of these 48-card decks are shuffled together and dealt from a regular blackjack shoe.

Face Cards

Each face card (jack, queen, and king) has a numerical value of 10. In a standard blackjack deck, there are 16 ten-value cards, while in a Spanish 21 deck, there are only 12 ten-value cards. As a result, the dealer will bust less often and the players will make blackjacks less often. Since the effectiveness of doubling down depends on the prevalence of 10-value cards, its benefit to the player has been degraded.

Aces

An ace may be valued 1 or 11, as the player wishes. An ace is usually valued 11 if the remaining cards in the hand add up to 10 or less, otherwise it is counted as a 1.

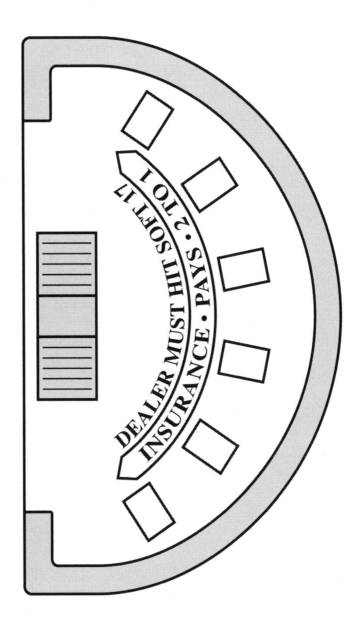

Figure 5 - Typical Spanish 21 Table

Soft Hand

A hand containing an ace that can be valued 11 without the total count going over 21. All other hands are considered *hard*. A soft hand has the property that it can always take a hit without going over 21, because the value of the ace can be changed to 1, if necessary.

Hard hand

A hand that does not contain an ace or a hand in which the ace (or aces) can only be counted as 1, without going over 21.

The Deal

The game begins when all the players have placed their bets. Most Spanish 21 games have a $5 or higher minimum bet requirement. The dealer distributes two face-up cards to each player and gives herself one face-down and one face-up card. The dealer's upcard gives you an important clue in making the decision on whether to take a hit or to stand. When the player's cards are dealt face up, as in Spanish 21, you are not allowed to touch any cards. The dealer does all the card handling.

Blackjack

A *blackjack* is a hand consisting of an ace plus any ten-value card. If the dealer's upcard is an ace or a ten-value card (jack, queen, or king), she peeks at her downcard to see if she has a blackjack. If she does, the hand is terminated and everyone loses automatically unless you also have a blackjack. Whenever you get a blackjack, you win regardless of what the dealer has, and are paid 3 to 2 odds. This is a nice improvement over standard blackjack where, if you match the dealer's blackjack, it is just a push. In Spanish 21, you will be dealt an average of one blackjack in about 24 hands. This is not as good as standard six-deck blackjack, however, where you can expect to get one blackjack in about 18 hands.

PLAYER'S TURN

If the dealer does not have a blackjack, when it is your turn you have to decide how to play your hand. The various choices available have to be communicated to the dealer with hand signals or by increasing your wager. This is done in rotation, starting from the first player to the left of the dealer, known in the trade as *first base*. The available options are as follows:

Hit

If you are not satisfied with the two-card count, you may draw additional cards, one-by-one. This is called taking a hit. Indicate this to the dealer by tapping or scratching the felt, with a finger, directly behind the cards. You may hit as many times as you want, so long as you don't go over 21. If the card count exceeds 21, your bet is lost. This is called *busting*. If you bust, the dealer will immediately remove your bet and your cards from the layout.

Stand

When you are satisfied with the card count and don't want any more hits, you may stand. Signal this intention to the dealer by waving your hand, palm down, over the cards.

Split

Whenever you are dealt a pair, you have the option of splitting the cards into two separate hands. Indicate this to the dealer by placing a second wager alongside your original bet. It must be for the same amount as the original bet. Before acting on your signal, the dealer may ask if you intend to double (see below) or split. With a pair of fives, for instance, most dealers know that splitting is not good strategy, but doubling may be appropriate.

When it is clear that you are splitting, the dealer will give you two more cards, one on each of your original cards, so that you are now playing two hands of two cards each. In most casinos, if you are splitting aces, those two are the only cards you will get. For all other pairs, you may hit each of the hands as many times as you wish.

Resplit

If, when you split a pair, one or both of the cards you get from the dealer are the same rank as the original pair, you may split again. This is called *resplitting*. For instance, if you split a pair of eights and got another eight, you could resplit into three hands. In Spanish 21, you may split cards of the same rank up to four times. In standard blackjack, some casinos do not allow resplitting.

Double Down

You may double down on any hand by placing another wager up to the amount of your original bet. Place the new wager alongside your other bet(s), just as for splitting. When you double down, you receive only one additional card from the dealer. This is good strategy when your hand reaches a total of 10 or 11 and the dealer is showing a low card. Because of the prevalence of ten-value cards in the deck, you are hoping to get a 20 or 21.

In Spanish 21, you may double down on your original two-card hand, after you have taken one or more hits, or after a split. When you double down, however, that hand does not qualify for a bonus. Although the doubling down rules are more liberal than in standard blackjack, because of the fewer ten-value cards, it is not done as often.

Double Down Rescue

If, after getting a double down card you don't like the resulting hand, you may take back (rescue) the doubled portion of your wager and forfeit your original bet. This can only be done if the hand did not go over 21. Assuming you used proper doubling strategy in the first place, this is not a recommended option.

Surrender

If you don't like what you see when you are dealt the first two cards, you may fold (surrender) your hand and forfeit half of your bet. If you decide to surrender, simply tell the dealer that you are surrendering. Once you take the first hit, you lose this option. You also lose it if the dealer has a blackjack, in which case you lose your entire bet. In a few specific instances, surrender is a useful option.

Insurance

If the dealer's upcard is an ace, the dealer will call out, "Insurance", and you are offered the opportunity to place an insurance side bet. You do this by putting up to half the amount of your original bet on the layout area marked INSURANCE. If, after peeking at the downcard, the dealer turns up a blackjack, any insurance bets are paid off at 2 to 1 odds. If the dealer does not have a blackjack, the insurance side bet is lost. From a player's strategy standpoint, this is not a good wager. Don't do it.

DEALER'S TURN

When the player's turns are over and each of them has stood, folded, or busted, it is the dealer's turn to play. The dealer then exposes her down card and has to play her hand in accordance with the following rule: With a card count of 16 or less, the dealer must take a hit, and with a count of 17 or more, the dealer must stand. The one exception occurs when the dealer's hand contains an ace. If the count is a soft 17, the dealer must take a hit. This exception, which is often not applied in standard blackjack, is unfavorable to the player because it increases the house edge by about 0.2%. If the dealer busts, all players who are still active automatically win.

TABLE ETIQUETTE

Experienced blackjack players will find that Spanish 21 is essentially similar to standard blackjack, except that the player's cards are dealt face up. If you are new to Spanish 21 and blackjack, just watch what the other players are doing and try to do the same. Should you make a mistake in table protocol, the dealer will politely correct you.

The first thing you have to do is place your wager. Put the chip(s) directly on the betting spot as soon as the dealer has collected all the cards from the previous hand. If you are slow in doing this, you may get bypassed on the deal. Most dealers, however, will simply remind you by pointing at the empty bet circle.

As soon as you see your two cards and the dealer's upcard, make a quick decision as to what action to take. Quickness is especially important if you are in the first-base position at the table, and you don't want everyone staring at you. If you know the strategy well, this should not be a problem.

Remember that you are not allowed to touch your cards or your original bet. The dealer does all the card handling. If you double down or split, never place additional chips on top of your original bet. Always put them alongside.

Don't signal the dealer until it is your turn. Make your hand signals clear so your intentions are not misunderstood. When you get paid off, be sure to pull back the chips or they may become your wager for the next round.

3 — THE PAYOFFS
Blackjacks, 21 counts, and bonus hands are paid as soon as they occur. Other non-busted player's hands are paid after the dealer has finished hitting her hand per the house rules. To reiterate, the dealer has to hit on 16 and stand on 17. If the dealer goes over 21, all non-busted hands (that haven't yet been paid) are winners and are paid off at even money.

STANDARD PAYOFFS
Blackjack
When you have a blackjack, you get paid 3 to 2 odds even if the dealer also has a blackjack. That is, for a $10 wager, you will win $15 and keep your original bet of $10.

21 Count
If your hand has a count of 21, you win even money. This is true even if the dealer has 21. The only way you can lose is if the dealer has a blackjack. There are no pushes on a 21 hand. Certain 21 hands pay better than even money. This is covered below, in the section on bonuses.

Other Hands
In general, when your non-busted hand has a higher count than the dealer has, you get paid even money. That is, a $10 wager wins an additional $10. When your hand is the same as the dealer's, it is considered a push and no money changes hands. When your count is less than the dealer's, you lose your bet.

BONUSES
Bonus 21
Certain non-doubled 21 hands pay bonuses as high as 3 to 1. The bonuses are always paid except when the dealer has a blackjack. These bonus hands are as follows:

• A 5-card hand with an exact count of 21, pays 3 to 2.
• A 6-card hand with an exact count of 21, pays 2 to 1.
• A 7-card (or more) hand with an exact count of 21, pays 3 to 1.
• A 3-card hand of a 6, 7, 8 with mixed suits, pays 3 to 2.
• A 3-card hand of a 6, 7, 8, all of the same suit, pays 2 to 1.
• A 3-card hand of a 6, 7, 8, all of which are spades, pays 2 to 1.
• A 3-card hand of all sevens with mixed suits, pays 3 to 2.
• A 3-card hand of all sevens of the same suit, pays 2 to 1.
• A 3-card hand of all sevens of spades, pays 2 to 1.

The bonuses were carefully designed to get you to take hits that risk busting your hand. To get the bonus for the five, six, or seven card hands, the count has to be exactly 21. You will find that this is not an easy task to accomplish because of the very high probability of busting. If you have the start of a 6-7-8 or 7-7-7 hand and are trying for the bonus, you may have to take a hit when you don't want to.

The following table summarizes the nine bonus hands described above:

BONUS 21 PAYTABLE	
HAND	**PAYS**
Five-card 21	3 to 2
Six-card 21	2 to 1
Seven-card 21	3 to 1
6-7-8 Mixed suits	3 to 2
6-7-8 Suited	2 to 1
6-7-8 Spades	3 to 1
7-7-7 Mixed suits	3 to 2
7-7-7 Suited	2 to 1
7-7-7 Spades	3 to 1

SUPER BONUS

When you get a 7-7-7 hand, all of the same suit, and the dealer's upcard is a seven of any suit, you will be paid a super bonus and all other players at the table will be paid an "envy" bonus. If you wagered $5 to $24, the super bonus pays $1000. If you bet $25 or more, the super bonus is $5000.

In either case, an envy bonus of $50 is paid to every other player at the table. *The super and the envy bonuses do not pay off if your hand was split or doubled.* In some casinos the super bonus payoff is handled a little differently. You get $1000 for each $5 bet increment, up to a maximum of $5000 for a $25 bet. For instance, if you wagered $15, the bonus would be $3000. No matter what you wagered, the other players still get their $50 envy bonus.

4 – PLAYING STRATEGY

Unlike standard blackjack, Spanish 21 is a negative expectation game. There is no playing strategy that will overcome the house edge and make the game profitable for the player. Sure, you can learn to count cards and reduce the house edge, but to swing it to a positive expectation is not easy to do. Spanish 21 was specifically designed to thwart card counters (more on this later).

Whether or not you count cards, when playing this game you must use some reasonable strategy or you will lose consistently. The problem is that the basic strategy rules for standard blackjack do not work very well for Spanish 21. Experienced blackjack players should be aware that they have to learn a new set of strategy rules if they expect to last very long at a Spanish 21 table.

The basic strategy for standard blackjack is not very simple. In Spanish 21, the basic strategy is not any simpler, just different. The changes in strategy are mainly due to the 25% fewer 10-value cards in the deck. The bonuses for certain 21-count hands also contribute to the variation in strategy rules.

A simplified strategy was devised for those casual players that would rather not memorize the full basic strategy table. If you are familiar with the basic strategy for standard blackjack, you will find the simple strategy to be similar, yet there are some significant differences.

A SIMPLE STRATEGY

The simple strategy table is a condensed and simplified version of the full basic strategy table shown later in this chapter. Before sitting down at a Spanish 21 game, you should try to learn the following rules:

SIMPLE PLAYING STRATEGY
for Spanish 21

Hard Hands	Dealer's Up	Action
17 thru 21	All	Stand
15 & 16	7 thru A	Hit
15 & 16	2 thru 6	Stand
12 thru 14	All	Hit
10 & 11	8 thru A	Hit
10 & 11	2 thru 7	Double
10 & 11 w/ 5+ cards	2 thru 7	Hit
5 thru 9	All	Hit

Soft Hands	Dealer's Up	Action
18 thru 21	All	Stand
13 thru 17	All	Hit

Pairs	Dealer's Up	Action
A-A & 8-8	All	Split
9-9	2 thru 9	Split
6-6 & 7-7	2 thru 7	Split
2-2 & 3-3	2 thru 7	Split
Other pairs	Do not split, play as hard hands	

True, these strategy rules are oversimplified, but they will keep you going until you learn the full basic strategy. To be sure you understand the table, we will do a quick run-through.

HARD HANDS

It is easy to remember that you always stand on good counts of 17 through 21. It is also easy to remember that for counts of 5 through 9 you always take a hit, because you can't bust.

It may be harder to remember to hit all 12-count through 14-count hands, because this is something that isn't done in standard black jack. In Spanish 21, however, the reduced number of ten-value cards makes it safer to hit such hands. Although it is risky to hit 15-count and 16-count hands, you have to assume that a dealer showing a 7 or higher already has you beat, so you have little choice.

You normally double on a 10 or 11 when the dealer shows a low card. If you have 5 or 6 cards in your hand, however, you should take a hit and go for the bonus.

SOFT HANDS

Even though you can't bust a soft hand, you should stand on a count of 18 through 21 because those hands are hard to improve. For a count of 17 or less, always take a hit.

PAIR SPLITTING

This is pretty easy to remember. Always split aces and eights. Never split fours, fives, or tens. Split others when the dealer shows a low card.

Aces are split because 2- or 12-count hands are not good, but hitting just a single ace can often result in a very good hand or even a blackjack. Eights are split because a count of 16 is an awful hand, while hitting a single eight can often result in an 18.

Fours or fives are never split because hitting an 8-count or 10-count can produce a good hand. Tens are never split, because you don't want to destroy a 20-count hand, which is a winner most of the time.

Split twos, threes, sixes, sevens, and nines when the dealer shows a low card. This way, you will win on two hands if the dealer busts, which will happen over one-third of the time. Whenever you don't split a pair, it should be played like a normal hard hand.

THE BASIC STRATEGY

Although the simpler strategy table works well for most recreational players, when you are ready to exert that extra effort needed to cut the house advantage down to the minimum, you have to learn the basic strategy. Although it is similar to the basic strategy for standard blackjack, there are significant differences that should not be overlooked.

The basic strategy for Spanish 21 that is presented in this book was originally developed by the late Lenny Frome. It is still the best around, so we can't do any better for our readers.

BASIC STRATEGY FOR SPANISH 21

- DEALER'S UPCARD -

HARD

	2	3	4	5	6	7	8	9	Face	Ace
18-21	S	S	S	S	S	S	S	S	S	S
17	S	S	S	S	S	S	Sh6	Sh6	Sh6	Sur
16	Sh5	Sh6	Sh6	S	S	H	H	H	H	Sur
15	Sh4	Sh5	Sh5	Sh6	Sh6	H	H	H	H	H
14	H	H	Sh4	Sh5	Sh5	H	H	H	H	H
13	H	H	H	Sh5	Sh4	H	H	H	H	H
12	H	H	H	H	H	H	H	H	H	H
11	Dh4	Dh5	Dh5	Dh5	Dh5	Dh4	Dh4	H	H	H
10	Dh5	Dh5	Dh6	D	D	Dh4	H	H	H	H
9	H	H	H	H	Dh3	H	H	H	H	H
5 - 8	H	H	H	H	H	H	H	H	H	H

SOFT

	2	3	4	5	6	7	8	9	Face	Ace
19-21	S	S	S	S	S	S	S	S	S	S
18	Sh4	Sh4	Dh4	Dh5	Dh6	S	Sh4	H	H	H
17	H	H	Dh3	Dh4	Dh5	H	H	H	H	H
16	H	H	H	H	Dh4	H	H	H	H	H
13-15	H	H	H	H	H	H	H	H	H	H

PAIRS

	2	3	4	5	6	7	8	9	Face	Ace
A-A	Spl	Spl	Spl	Spl	Spl	Spl	Spl	Spl	Spl	Spl
10-10	S	S	S	S	S	S	S	S	S	S
9-9	S	Spl	Spl	Spl	Spl	S	Spl	Spl	S	S
8-8	Spl	Spl	Spl	Spl	Spl	Spl	Spl	Spl	Spl	Sur
7-7	Spl	Spl	Spl	Spl	Spl	Spl	H	H	H	H
6-6	H	H	Spl	Spl	Spl	H	H	H	H	H
5-5	D	D	D	D	D	D	H	H	H	H
4-4	H	H	H	H	H	H	H	H	H	H
3-3	H	Spl	Spl	Spl	Spl	Spl	H	H	H	H
2-2	H	Spl	Spl	Spl	Spl	Spl	H	H	H	H

Numbers in the leftmost column represent the player's hand

H = Hit **S** = Stand **D** = Double **Spl** = Split **Sur** = Surrender
Sh3, Sh4, Sh5, Sh6 = STAND, except HIT if hand contains 3, 4, 5, or 6 cards
Dh3, Dh4, Dh5, Dh6 = DOUBLE, except HIT if hand contains 3, 4, 5, or 6 cards

CARD COUNTING

As most blackjack players know, a proficient card counter can overcome the house edge and even swing it to his advantage. Ever since Dr. Edward Thorp published his groundbreaking book "Beat the Dealer" in 1962, the casinos have been annoyed to no end that some players could actually get the better of them.

If it wasn't for the fact that the increased popularity of blackjack has produced huge profits, the casinos might have introduced drastic rule changes or even eliminated the game entirely. As it was, few players bothered to master the many counting techniques that have been published over the years. In fact, most people play blackjack so carelessly that the casinos never have to worry about losing money.

However, the casino industry vowed never to introduce a new game that had any possibility of being beaten honestly.Enter Spanish 21. As a major variation of standard blackjack, it was designed to intrigue blackjack players and, at the same time, thwart any attempts to gain an advantage by counting cards.

This goal was fully accomplished. The game's designer even eliminated the possibility of player cheating by having the dealer do all the card handling.

Yes, you can still count cards, but the count very rarely gets good. This is the result of fewer ten-value cards. When perfect playing strategy is used, the house edge can get as low as 0.8%, which is still too high for most expert counters to overcome. In theory, the house edge could be overcome by making very large (and very obvious) bet swings, but this is simply not practical.

Sorry, but your best bet is to stick to the basic strategy and enjoy the game.

CONCLUSION

With its more favorable payoff rules, most blackjack players consider Spanish 21 to be a pleasant change. Some of the annoyances of standard casino blackjack have been eliminated. The big danger is to blackjack players who think they can use the same basic strategy that they know so well. The casinos bank on this and have been raking it in from those unaware players.

With proper playing strategy, however, the house edge can get as low as 0.8%, which is not bad. It allows your bankroll to survive for some time while you are waiting for that big lucky streak.

VII. PAI GOW

OVERVIEW

This is not a new game at all, but is relatively new in Nevada casinos. Pai Gow is a very ancient Chinese domino game, and is only offered in a few of the larger casinos. It is rare to see a non-Chinese player at a Pai Gow table—and for very good reason. To most non-Chinese, the game is almost incomprehensible and the strategy is elusive. Furthermore, the minimum bet requirement is typically $25 or higher—a $100 minimum not being unusual. To play a complicated, unfamiliar game at that betting level is not wise.

There are few English-language books describing Pai Gow, one of the best of which is by Michael Musante (*Pai Gow - Chinese Dominoes,* GBC Press, Las Vegas). If you really want to try the game, be sure to get his book first. To quote Mr. Musante:

> *When I was first learning the game, I asked an elderly Chinese gentleman, "What is required to really know the game of Pai Gow?" He replied: "First of all you must be Chinese, and then you must be a thousand years old."*

My advice is to avoid the game. If you are tempted to try, you will find the dealer and other players to be very helpful. However, you will not fully comprehend the explanations and they will eat you alive. You will be much better off playing the Americanized version called Pai Gow Poker.

VIII. CASINO RED DOG

OVERVIEW

This is an old American game that dates back to the gambling halls of the early West and was also played extensively as a private game, especially by newspaper reporters. Because the game became such an easy mark for cheaters, it eventually fell out of popularity.

Some casinos revived the old Red Dog a number of years ago, but changed the game so that it is significantly different from the original. We call this version *Casino Red Dog,* and it falls in the general category of New Games. Casino Red Dog never became very popular, and it is hard to find in the newer casinos.

The casino version is quite simple. After an initial ante, the dealer places two cards face-up on the table. The players may then raise their bets if they think a third card will fall between the first two cards in rank. The cards are valued 2 through 14, with jack = 11, queen = 12, king = 13, and ace = 14. That is, deuce is low and ace is high.

The spread is the number of ranks between the two dealt cards. For instance, if the two cards are 5 and 9, the spread is 3. All players are in the same boat. They all win if the third card dealt falls *between* the first two cards, otherwise they lose.

PAYOUTS

The payouts are according to the following schedule:

CASINO RED DOG PAYTABLE	
Spread of 1	Pays 5 to 1
Spread of 2	Pays 4 to 1
Spread of 3	Pays 2 to 1
Spread of 4 thru 11	Pays 1 to 1

A consecutive hand, such as 8 and 9 is considered a tie, and the dealer does not draw a third card. This is a push and the players neither win nor lose.

For a pair hand, such as 8 and 8, the dealer automatically draws a third card, and the players do not get an opportunity to raise. If the third card is the same rank as the first two, the players get paid 11 to 1 on their ante bets. If the third card is different, it is a push.

CONCLUSION

In Casino Red Dog you don't get to handle any cards and the only decision is whether or not to raise your bet. If you can find the game, the best strategy is to raise only when the two-card spread is seven or greater. Even with the correct strategy, however, the casino edge is about 3.5%.

IX. SIC BO

OVERVIEW

This is another Asian game that is a fixture in the casinos of Macao and has taken up residence in Las Vegas and Atlantic City. It is played on a rectangular table with a layout consisting of numbers and dice faces that represent all the combinations that can be made with three dice. The players try to predict the outcome of a roll of three dice by placing their wagers on appropriate places of the layout.

After a short betting period, the dice are shaken and rolled by the dealer using a special dice box. The winning numbers and combinations light up on the table surface. Losing bets are raked in and the winning bets are paid off. The players then place their bets for the next roll of the dice.

This is a pure luck game with no strategy except to choose bets with a reasonable house edge—and there aren't many of those. Most of the bet combinations give the house an advantage of 10 to 30%, and one bet carries an outrageous 47-percent edge. To top it off, you don't even get to roll the dice!

CONCLUSION

If you *must* lay down a bet, look for the squares marked SMALL and BIG, which have a house edge of only 2.7%—the lowest on the table. When you bet on SMALL, you win even money if the three dice add up to a total of 4 through 10. You win on BIG when the dice add up to a total of 11 through 17. So, bet either SMALL or BIG or just stand around and watch the table light up. Any other course of action (other than walking away) would be a foolish risk of money.

X. WAR

OVERVIEW

This is a silly little game offered by many of the larger casinos. It is similar to the one by the same name that you played as a small child on a rainy day when you couldn't find anything better to do.

Most tables have a $5 minimum bet. After shuffling a single deck (oddly, some casinos use a six-deck shoe), the dealer buries a card and then deals out one card to you and one to herself. All the cards are dealt face up. If the rank of your card is higher than the dealer's, you win; if the dealer's card is higher, you lose. Suits have no relative value. The payoff is even money, that is, if you wager $5 and you win, you will get back your original bet plus $5.

Whenever your card is the same rank as the dealer's, you have the option of folding and forfeiting half of your bet or going for a playoff by putting up an additional wager equal to your original bet. The playoff is called "going to war."

If you decide to put up the additional bet, the dealer will match your bet and deal out two more cards, one for you, and one for her. If you win on the second two cards, you will get back both your bets plus the dealer's matching bet. This amounts to a push on your first bet and an even money payoff on your second bet.

If you lose, you will lose all your bets. If the second pair of cards is also a tie, you win the hand and get a bonus equal to your original bet.

Before each hand is dealt, you may also make a side bet that you and the dealer will have a tie. If you win that bet, the payoff is 10 to 1. The actual probability of getting a tie is 1 chance in 17, so the house takes a ridiculous edge of 35% on this wager.

Let's say your first bet was $10 and the play resulted in a tie. If you fold, it will cost you $5 (half of your bet). If you quit now (strongly adviseable), the house edge is a reasonable 2.9%. If, instead, you decide to put up a second bet of $10, the dealer will match it with $10 and deal two more cards. Should you lose this round, you lose both bets ($20). If you win, you get back both of your bets ($20) plus the $10 put up by the dealer for the second bet. You also win if there is another tie, in which case you will be paid a bonus of $10.

Note that the casino no longer pays even money when you go to war. You are risking $20 for a chance to win back only $10. Of course you get a $10 "bonus" for a second tie, but your chances of getting a tie are only 1 in 17. Thus, in this playoff round, the house edge skyrockets to 17%.

CONCLUSION

Understandably, this game is not very popular. Most War tables just sit there with a bored dealer and no players. It is a dull little game that entails no playing strategy (other than not playing ties). The house advantage is exhorbitant, and it doesn't even have a big jackpot to keep you interested.

XI. STRATEGY CHARTS

As a convenience to the reader, strategy charts for the five major games covered in this book have been replicated on the following pages. The charts are on three two-page spreads to simplify reproduction. By opening the book flat on a flat-bed copier or scanner, you can reproduce one or more charts on a single 8.5- x 11-inch sheet.

After making the copies, fold the sheets for best convenience, or cut out the individual charts. Don't hesitate to bring strategy charts into a casino, but try to be a little subtle about it. If casino personnel don't like to see them used, they will mention it to you. Attitudes vary from casino to casino.

CARIBBEAN STUD POKER
Simple Playing Strategy

Rule 1: Never ante more than the table minimum.
Rule 2: Never bet on the progressive jackpot.
Rule 3: Call if hand contains an Ace-King-Queen or better. Otherwise, fold.

CARIBBEAN STUD POKER
Perfect Playing Strategy

Rule 1: Never ante more than the table minimum.
Rule 2: Bet $1 on progressive jackpot only when the meter exceeds the positive expectation breakpoint.
Rule 3: Call if hand contains an **Ace-King-Jack-9-5** or better. Otherwise, fold.
Rule 4: Ignore the dealer's upcard.

THREE CARD POKER
A Perfectly Simple Strategy

Rule 1: Ante the table minimum.
Rule 2: Pair Plus bet is optional.
Rule 3: Call your hand if it contains a Queen or better. Otherwise, fold.

LET IT RIDE
Perfect Playing Strategy

Rule 1: Never bet more than the table minimum.

Rule 2: Never place a $1 bonus bet.

Rule 3: Three-Card Strategy — Let the first bet ride if your initial 3-card hand contains any of the following: Any paying hand (pair of tens or better) A possible royal flush A possible straight flush

Rule 4: Four-Card Strategy — Let the second bet ride if your 4-card hand (including the first community card) contains any of the following: Any paying hand (pair of tens or better) All cards of the same suit An open-ended straight

PAI GOW POKER
Simple Playing Strategy

General Rule 1: Set the 2-card hand as high as possible without compromising the 5-card hand.

General Rule 2: Break-even for 2 cards is **A-8**. Break-even for 5 cards is **J-J**. Try to exceed break-even on both hands.

Specific common hands:

High card — Two-card the 2nd- and 3rd-highest cards.

One pair — Two-card the 2 highest singletons.

Two pairs — Without singleton Ace: Always split pairs. — With singleton Ace: Split J-J, 7-7 or better.

Three-of-a-kind — Split A-A-A. Do not split other triplets.

Straight— Five-card the lowest 5 cards in straight.

Flush — Five-card the lowest 5 cards in flush. Split flush, as necessary, to meet Rule 2.

PAI GOW POKER
Long Playing Strategy

High card — A hand consisting of seven unrelated cards (singletons), with no flush, no straight, and no pairs.
>Two-card the second- and third-highest cards.
>If the two highest cards are A-K or A-Q, two-card the second- and fourth-highest cards

One pair — Five singletons with no flush and no straight. This is the most common hand in Pai Gow Poker.
>Two-card the two highest singletons.

Two pairs — Three singletons with no flush and no straight. To split means: two-card the smaller pair and five-card the remaining cards.
>High pair is A-A: Split.
>High pair is K-K: Split.
>>Except if low pair is 5-5 thru 2-2 with A-J or higher: Two-card the highest singletons.
>High pair is Q-Q: Split.
>>Except if low pair is 9-9 thru 2-2 with A-J or higher: Two-card the highest singletons.
>High pair is J-J: Split.
>>Except with A-J or higher: Two-card the highest singletons.
>High pair is 9-9 or 10-10: Split.
>>Except with singleton ace: Two-card the highest singletons.
>High pair is 6-6 to 8-8: Split.
>>Except with singleton king or better: Two-card the highest singletons.
>High pair is 3-3 to 5-5: Split.
>>Except with singleton queen or better: Two-card the highest singletons.

Three pairs — Plus one singleton.
>Two-card the highest pair.

Three of a kind — Four singletons with no flush and no straight. To split means: break the triplet and five-card the resulting pair.
>A-A-A: Split and two-card one ace plus the highest singleton.
>K-K-K with J-10 or higher: Two-card the highest singletons.
>K-K-K with J-9 or lower: Split and two-card one king plus the highest singleton.
>Q-Q-Q: Two-card the highest singletons.

Straight — Two singletons with no flush and no pair. May include the joker.
>Five-card the straight
>For a six- or seven-card straight, five-card the lowest-value straight.

Flush — Two singletons with no straight and no pair. May include the joker.
>Five-card the flush
>For a six- or seven-card flush, five-card the lowest-value flush.

Straight or flush, with external pair — The pair is external to the straight or flush.
>Two-card the pair, five-card the straight or flush.

Straight and included pair, no joker — One of the pair is shared by the straight.
Six- or seven-card straight: Five-card the lowest five cards of the straight.
Hand contains no Ace: Five-card the straight.
Ace-high straight with Q-Q, J-J, or 10-10: Five-card the pair and two-card the A-K.
Ace-high straight with A-A or K-K: Five-card the straight.

Straight and included pair, with joker — One of the pair is shared by the straight.
Ace or joker not needed to complete straight: Five-card the straight.
Ace-joker pair needed to complete ace-high straight: Five-card the ace and joker plus three lowest singletons.
Ace-joker pair needed to complete ace-low straight: Five-card the straight.
Jack-high (or higher) joker straight: Five-card the pair.
Ten-high (or lower) joker straight: Five-card the straight.

Flush and included pair — One or two of the pair are shared by the flush.
Six- or seven-card flush: Five-card the lowest five cards of the flush.
Ace and/or joker not needed to complete flush: Five-card the flush.
Ace and/or joker needed to complete flush: Five-card the pair if second-highest card is 10 or better and pair is 10-10 or better. Otherwise, five-card the flush.

Straight and flush or straight flush — No pairs.
Five-card the straight or the flush, whichever leaves the highest two-card hand.
The rule is the same for a straight flush or royal.

Straight and flush and one pair — Or straight flush.
If possible, two-card the pair and five-card the straight or flush or straight flush.
If pair is included, use above rules for straight or flush with included pair.

Straight or flush and two pairs — Or straight flush.
If possible, two-card one of the pairs and five-card the straight or flush.
If both pairs are included, split the straight or flush and use above rules for two pairs.

Full house — Plus two singletons. May include the joker.
Split the full house and two-card the pair.

Three of a kind plus three of a kind — Plus one singleton.
Two-card a pair from the higher triplet and five-card the lower triplet.

Four of a kind — Plus three singletons.
A-A-A-A or K-K-K-K: Split the quad and two-card a pair.
Q-Q-Q-Q or J-J-J-J: With a singleton ace, five-card the quad. Otherwise split.
10-10-10-10 or 9-9-9-9: With a king or higher, five-card the quad. Otherwise split.
8-8-8-8 or 7-7-7-7: With queen or higher, five-card the quad. Otherwise split.
6-6-6-6 or lower: Five-card the quad.

Four of a kind plus one pair — Plus one singleton.
Five-card the quad and two-card the pair.
Exception: If quad is Q-Q-Q-Q or higher *and* pair is 4-4 or lower, two-card two of the quad and five-card two pairs.

Four of a kind plus three of a kind — No singletons.
Two-card the highest pair and five-card either a quad or a full house.

Five aces — Plus two singletons.
Two-card a pair of aces.

SPANISH 21
Simple Playing Strategy

Hard Hands	Dealer's Up	Action
17 thru 21	All	Stand
15 & 16	7 thru A	Hit
15 & 16	2 thru 6	Stand
12 thru 14	All	Hit
10 & 11	8 thru A	Hit
10 & 11	2 thru 7	Double
10 & 11 w/ 5+ cards	2 thru 7	Hit
5 thru 9	All	Hit

Soft Hands	Dealer's Up	Action
18 thru 21	All	Stand
13 thru 17	All	Hit

Pairs	Dealer's Up	Action
A-A & 8-8	All	Split
9-9	2 thru 9	Split
6-6 & 7-7	2 thru 7	Split
2-2 & 3-3	2 thru 7	Split
Other pairs	Do not split—play as hard hands	

BASIC STRATEGY FOR SPANISH 21

- DEALER'S UPCARD -

HARD

	2	3	4	5	6	7	8	9	Face	Ace
18-21	S	S	S	S	S	S	S	S	S	S
17	S	S	S	S	S	S	Sh6	Sh6	Sh6	Sur
16	Sh5	Sh6	Sh6	S	S	H	H	H	H	Sur
15	Sh4	Sh5	Sh5	Sh6	Sh6	H	H	H	H	H
14	H	H	Sh4	Sh5	Sh5	H	H	H	H	H
13	H	H	H	Sh5	Sh4	H	H	H	H	H
12	H	H	H	H	H	H	H	H	H	H
11	Dh4	Dh5	Dh5	Dh5	Dh5	Dh4	Dh4	H	H	H
10	Dh5	Dh5	Dh6	D	D	Dh4	H	H	H	H
9	H	H	H	H	Dh3	H	H	H	H	H
5 - 8	H	H	H	H	H	H	H	H	H	H

SOFT

	2	3	4	5	6	7	8	9	Face	Ace
19-21	S	S	S	S	S	S	S	S	S	S
18	Sh4	Sh4	Dh4	Dh5	Dh6	S	Sh4	H	H	H
17	H	H	Dh3	Dh4	Dh5	H	H	H	H	H
16	H	H	H	H	Dh4	H	H	H	H	H
13-15	H	H	H	H	H	H	H	H	H	H

PAIRS

	2	3	4	5	6	7	8	9	Face	Ace
A-A	Spl	Spl	Spl	Spl	Spl	Spl	Spl	Spl	Spl	Spl
10-10	S	S	S	S	S	S	S	S	S	S
9-9	S	Spl	Spl	Spl	Spl	S	Spl	Spl	S	S
8-8	Spl	Spl	Spl	Spl	Spl	Spl	Spl	Spl	Spl	Sur
7-7	Spl	Spl	Spl	Spl	Spl	Spl	H	H	H	H
6-6	H	H	Spl	Spl	Spl	H	H	H	H	H
5-5	D	D	D	D	D	D	H	H	H	H
4-4	H	H	H	H	H	H	H	H	H	H
3-3	H	Spl	Spl	Spl	Spl	Spl	H	H	H	H
2-2	H	Spl	Spl	Spl	Spl	Spl	H	H	H	H

Numbers in the leftmost column represent the player's hand

H = Hit   **S** = Stand   **D** = Double   **Spl** = Split   **Sur** = Surrender
Sh3, Sh4, Sh5, Sh6 = STAND, except HIT if hand contains 3, 4, 5, or 6 cards
Dh3, Dh4, Dh5, Dh6 = DOUBLE, except HIT if hand contains 3, 4, 5, or 6 cards

XII. GLOSSARY

Ace — The highest-ranking card. May also be used as the lowest card in an A-2-3-4-5 straight or straight flush. In blackjack and Spanish 21, an ace may be valued either 1 or 11.

Ace high — A hand of unrelated cards that contains one ace.

Aces up — Two pairs, with one of the pairs being aces.

Aggregate limit — The maximum payout in any one game or hand.

Ante — In poker, the chips put into the pot before the initial deal. In Caribbean Stud and Three card Poker, the initial wager.

Bank — (a) The money on the table that is used by the dealer to pay winning bets. (b) The casino or the game operator. (c) Any person (including a player) who covers all the bets in a game.

Blackjack — In blackjack and Spanish 21, a hand consisting of an ace and a ten-value card. Also called a natural.

Blacks — Black casino checks with a value of $100 each.

Bleeder — A paranoid casino supervisor that worries about players winning. Also called a sweater.

Bug — A restricted joker that may be used only as an ace or a wild card to fill a flush, straight, or straight flush.

Bust — To exceed a count of 21 in blackjack or Spanish 21. Also called breaking.

Buy-in — (a) An exchange of a players currency for casino chips. (b) The amount of money a player gives the dealer for the chips.

Card mechanic — A skilled dealer who uses sleight-of-hand to cheat.

Check or cheque — Alternate term for Chip that is commonly used by casino personnel and professional gamblers.

Chip — A gaming token with an imprinted value that is used in place of real money at various table games in a casino. Chips may be redeemed for cash at the issuing casino. Also called house check, casino chip, or value chip. The terms Chip and Check are used interchangeably.

Commission — The percentage charged by the casino against winning hands in certain table games. A commission is typically 5% of the amount won. Also called vig, vigorish, or juice.

Dealer — The casino employee that operates the game and deals the cards.

Deuce — The two-spot card.

Double down — In blackjack and Spanish 21, to double your bet and receive one additional card. Also called double.

Edge — A statistical advantage. Usually the casino's advantage.

Even money — A wager that pays off at 1 to 1 odds, if it wins. That is, if a $5 bet wins, the original bet is returned along with an additional $5. Also called a flat bet or even money.

Expectation — The average amount that may be won or lost in a particular game over an extended period of play. Also called expectation of winning.

Face card — A jack, queen, or king. In blackjack and Spanish 21, all face cards count as 10.

Face down cards — Cards that are not exposed.

Face up cards — Cards that are exposed for all to see.

First base — The end seat at a gaming table, to the dealer's left. In blackjack and Spanish 21, this is the first hand that is dealt.

Five-of-a-kind — Five cards of the same rank. Since a standard deck has only four cards of each rank (one in each suit), this must include a designated wild card such as a deuce or a joker.

Floorman — A politically-incorrect term for a floor person.

Floor person — A floor supervisor.

Floor supervisor — A pit supervisor who reports to the pit boss. This is the person who watches dealers to assure that all losing bets are collected, winning bets are correctly paid, and nobody is cheating.

Flush — Five cards of the same suit.

Fold — In poker and poker-like games, to throw in your hand and drop out of play. This action forfeits any wagers made up to that point.

Four-card royal — Four of the five cards needed for a royal flush.

Four-flush — Four of the five cards needed for a flush; four cards of the same suit.

Four-of-a-kind — Four cards of the same rank.

Four straight — Four of the five cards needed for a straight.

Full house — Three-of-a-kind and a pair.

Garbage hand — A hand of no potential value, that does not even contain a low pair.

Greens — Green casino checks with a value of $25 each. Also called quarters.

Hand — The cards held by a player.

Hard hand — In blackjack and Spanish 21, a hand that either does not contain an ace or the ace can only be valued as 1, without going over 21.

High card — The highest card in a poker hand.

High pair — In jacks-or-better poker or video poker, a pair of jacks, queens, kings, or aces. In Let It Ride, a high pair also includes the ten.

Hit — In blackjack and Spanish 21, a request for another card.

Hole card — In stud poker and poker-like games, a card that is dealt face down. In blackjack and Spanish 21, the dealer's face down card.

House — The casino, the bank, or the game operator.

House edge — The difference between the actual odds and the payoff odds, usually stated as a percentage, which is the mathematical edge the house has over the player. Also called casino advantage, house percentage, or P.C.

House odds — The amount the house pays a winning bet, usually stated as an odds ratio such as 2 to 1. Also called odds paid or payoff odds.

Inside straight — Four of the five cards needed for a straight with a gap between the lowest and highest cards. The gap can be filled with a card of only one rank, or a total of four possible cards.

Insurance — In blackjack and Spanish 21, a side bet on whether or not the dealer has a blackjack when an ace is showing.

Joker — An extra card in the deck that is designated as a wild card. See *wild card*.

Layout — The imprinted surface of a gaming table displaying the positions of the bets.

Limit — See Table limit.

Martingale system — An even-money betting system in which the wager is doubled after every loss and is reduced to the initial bet after every win. Also called a doubling system.

Maximum — See Table limit.

Minimum — The smallest bet allowed at a table.

Natural — See Blackjack.

Nickels — See Reds.

Odds — The ratio of the number of ways to win versus the number of ways to lose.

Odds paid — See House odds.

Open-ended straight — Four cards in sequential rank which can become a straight if a card is added to either end. The straight can be completed with a card of either of two ranks, or a total of eight possible cards.

Outside straight — Same as an *open-ended straight*.

Pair — Two cards of the same rank.

Pat hand — A good hand, as dealt, that does not require a draw or a hit.

Payback — The total long-term winnings as a% of the total amount bet.

Payoff — The amount paid for a winning hand.

Payout — Same as *payoff*.

Payoff odds — See House odds.

P.C. — Gambler's abbreviation for percentage. See House edge.

Pit — The area behind a group of gaming tables that is restricted to casino employees.

Pit boss — The supervisor who is responsible for the tables in a specific pit or gaming area. The pit boss reports to the shift manager.

Push — A tie in which no money changes hands.

Quads — Another term for four-of-a-kind.

Quarters — See Greens.

Rank — The ordinal position of each card within a suit, determining its value. The lowest rank is the deuce and the highest is the ace. In a straight or a straight flush, an ace may also be used as the lowest card.

Reds — Red casino checks with a value of $5 each. Also called nickels.

Royal flush — A ten, jack, queen, king, and ace, all of the same suit.

Shoe — A box, at a dealer's left side, that holds several decks of shuffled cards which can be dealt out one at a time.

Showdown — The point in a conventional poker game when the hands of all active players are exposed and compared to determine who wins the pot.

Side bet — An optional second bet at a table game.

Single-ended straight — Four of the five cards needed for a straight in a sequence that is open at only one end. Specifically: A-2-3-4 or J-Q-K-A. The straight can be completed with a card of only one rank, or a total of four possible cards. Also called *inside straight*.

Soft hand — In blackjack and Spanish 21, a hand containing an ace which can be valued as either a 1 or 11 without going over 21.

Split — In blackjack and Spanish 21, to divide a pair into two separate hands.

Stand — In blackjack and Spanish 21, to not draw any more cards.

Straight — Five cards of consecutive rank, with mixed suits.

Straight flush — Five cards of consecutive rank, all of the same suit.

Suit — The name of one of the four families of 13 cards that make up a standard deck. The four suits are: spades, hearts, clubs, and diamonds.

Surrender — In Spanish 21 and some blackjack games, an option to drop out of play before taking a hit in return for forfeiting half the original wager.

Sweater — See Bleeder.

Table limit — The largest bet allowed at a table, which may be increased for a high roller. Also called limit or maximum.

Third base — The end seat at a gaming table, to the dealer's right. In blackjack and Spanish 21, this is the last hand that is dealt.

Three-of-a-kind — Three cards of the same rank.

Toke — Short for token, a gratuity given to the dealer. To comply with IRS rulings, tips are placed into toke boxes and periodically divided between all the dealers, after taxes have been withheld.

Triplets — Another term for three-of-a-kind. Also called *trips*.

Twenty-one — Another term for Blackjack.

Two pairs — Two cards of the same rank and two cards of another rank.

Upcard — A card that is dealt face up.

Vigorish — See Commission.

Wild card — A card, such as a joker, that may be designated as any other card to improve a hand, even if that card already appears in the hand. For instance, a hand containing four kings and a wild card would be considered five-of-a-kind.